TAROT
PREDICTION & DIVINATION

About the Author

Susyn Blair-Hunt is internationally known for her psychic tarot and astrology readings. A professional metaphysical consultant for more than twenty years, Blair-Hunt was named one of the top female psychic astrologers on the Internet by her peers. Visit her online at www.netreadings.com.

To Write to the Author

If you wish to contact the author or would like more information about this book, please write to the author in care of Llewellyn Worldwide and we will forward your request. Both the author and publisher appreciate hearing from you and learning of your enjoyment of this book and how it has helped you. Llewellyn Worldwide cannot guarantee that every letter written to the author can be answered, but all will be forwarded. Please write to:

Susyn Blair-Hunt
c/o Llewellyn Worldwide Ltd.
2143 Wooddale Drive
Woodbury, MN 55125-2989

Please enclose a self-addressed stamped envelope for reply,
or $1.00 to cover costs. If outside the U.S.A., enclose
an international postal reply coupon.

Many of Llewellyn's authors have websites with additional information and resources. For more information, please visit our website at:

www.llewellyn.com

TAROT
PREDICTION & DIVINATION

UNVEILING 3 LAYERS OF MEANING

SUSYN BLAIR-HUNT

Llewellyn Publications
Woodbury, Minnesota

Tarot Prediction & Divination: Unveiling Three Layers of Meaning © 2011 by Susyn Blair-Hunt. All rights reserved. No part of this book may be used or reproduced in any manner whatsoever, including Internet usage, without written permission from Llewellyn Publications, except in the case of brief quotations embodied in critical articles and reviews.

First Edition
First Printing, 2011

Cover design by Ellen Lawson
Cover images: curtains © PhotoDisc;
   grass and celestial sky/stars © BrandXPictures;
   texture © Corbis;
   landscape © iStockphoto.com/Iakov Kalinin
Cover Tarot card images from The Gilded Tarot by Ciro Marchetti
Editing by Laura Graves
Interior card diagrams by Llewellyn art department
Interior Tarot card images: The Gilded Tarot by Ciro Marchetti;
   Lo Scarabeo Tarot by Anna Lazzarini, reprinted by permission from Lo Scarabeo;
   Universal Tarot by Roberto De Angelis, reprinted by permission from Lo Scarabeo

Llewellyn is a registered trademark of Llewellyn Worldwide Ltd.

Library of Congress Cataloging-in-Publication Data
Blair-Hunt, Susyn, 1956–
  Tarot prediction & divination : unveiling 3 layers of meaning / Susyn Blair-Hunt.—1st ed.
    p. cm.
  Includes bibliographical references and index.
  ISBN 978-0-7387-2172-9 (alk. paper)
  1. Tarot. I. Title. II. Title: Tarot prediction and divination.
  BF1879.T2S64 2011
  133.3'2424—dc22
                       2010038828

Llewellyn Worldwide Ltd. does not participate in, endorse, or have any authority or responsibility concerning private business transactions between our authors and the public.

All mail addressed to the author is forwarded but the publisher cannot, unless specifically instructed by the author, give out an address or phone number.

Any Internet references contained in this work are current at publication time, but the publisher cannot guarantee that a specific location will continue to be maintained. Please refer to the publisher's website for links to authors' websites and other sources.

Llewellyn Publications
A Division of Llewellyn Worldwide Ltd.
2143 Wooddale Drive
Woodbury, MN 55125-2989
www.llewellyn.com

Printed in the United States of America

*To my parents, Audrey and Clarence,
who always encouraged me to explore unique paths in life.
Their faith and support inspired me to reach for the moon, dance in the stars,
and set my sights on the heavens, where my mother now resides.*

CONTENTS

Acknowledgements xi
Preface xiii

Introduction ... 1

1 • Beginner Readings ... 19
Yes or No Reading 21
Daily Advice Reading 29
The Illuminating Star Reading 37
The Reasons Reading 49
Birthday/Yearly Forecast Reading 59

2 • Intermediate Readings ... 79
Inverted Pyramid Reading 81
The Relationship Reading 99
Decision Trees Reading 113

The Veil/Truth Reading   129
　　Crossroads Reading   143

3 • Advanced Readings **157**
　　The Gypsy's Mirror Reading   159
　　Dream Interpretation Reading   173
　　Chakra/Health Reading   189
　　Past Life Reading   205
　　Channeling Chalice Reading   221

Appendix A: Tarot Keywords   233
Appendix B: Significators   237
Appendix C: Card Combinations   243
Appendix D: Timing Cards   273
Appendix E: Empowerment Guide   279

ACKNOWLEDGEMENTS

Special thanks to Michael Pitts, Joshua Hunt, Susan Winter Mills, Barbara Snowden, Louise Gilbertson, Dayanara Lodriguez, Dominique Jones, Julia Melges-Brenner, and Tammy Ahlbourn for their support, encouragement, and guidance.

PREFACE

So you've bought a deck of tarot cards, memorized their basic meanings, and want to know what to do next. Or perhaps you have been using the tarot for years, but feel the need to expand your abilities, refresh your perspective, and take your interpretive skills to the next level.

Tarot Prediction & Divination is designed to bring more depth and power to your readings as it takes you through the three dimensions of the Tarot: divinatory, therapeutic, and spiritual.

With fifteen original layouts, forty-five sample readings, and a series of unique correspondence charts, this book will teach you how to draw more insight from the tarot, making your readings more effective and profound.

Most tarot decks come with small instruction booklets that provide a brief interpretation of each card. They feature the Celtic Cross and at best, two or three additional layouts. As a result, many tarot enthusiasts adopt only one reading method and stick with it. After a time, this can become repetitive, ineffective, and limiting.

This book presents fifteen new layout options to enhance your readings, taking you from beginner to advanced readings and offering spreads that are subject specific to the question at hand. Throughout this book, the term "querent" will refer to the person asking the question, whether it is you or someone you are reading for.

Tarot Prediction & Divination's purpose is to offer expanded meanings and insights that give more versatility to the art of tarot interpretation. Through the example readings included with each layout, you will learn how to extract the predictive, therapeutic, and spiritual messages hidden within the cards. As you combine all three dimensions of the tarot, you'll be able to perform the most effective readings possible.

Unique in its approach, this guide uses visual literacy as a means to awaken your psychic abilities. This means that you can read not only the predictive messages, but also the healing and spiritual aspects contained in each card's image. You can read cards individually and/or as they relate to surrounding cards, finding a specific answer to your question.

As you prepare to explore *Tarot Prediction & Divination*, my wish is that your own path to enlightenment—as well as your ability to help others—will be empowered by this illuminating book.

Susyn Blair-Hunt, MsD

INTRODUCTION

The Role of Fortune Telling in Today's World

The term "fortune telling" often conjures up the image of a traveling carnival, or perhaps one of those seedy "Palm Readings" signs tucked away in an unsavory neighborhood. In truth, fortune telling takes many forms. Divination, psychic readings, and astrology are all practices that could fall under this general category, as they possess powerful transformative energies that can awaken and connect us to our spiritual centers.

In today's world, with so much going on around us, it's easy to get stuck in life's chaos. We operate on a physical plane, giving much credence to science, physics, and the tangible, which dulls our instincts. Unable to access or even trust our intuition, we can be overcome with fear at any given time. Fear is the great paralyzer, and, as portrayed in the Devil tarot card, can undermine our progress or make it impossible to connect with our spiritual selves and higher planes of being.

This is where the art of divination ("fortune telling") becomes essential. If we can gain affirmation and a sense of what is to come next or realize where we need to make changes, we can release our fears and relax. Once we do, Spirit will always bring us the answers we seek. Tarot's ritualistic aspects can loosen the grip of fear created by misunderstandings or spiritual short-sightedness, guiding us forward in the most effective way possible.

The tarot's purpose is not simply to provide us with all the answers, however. Its images offer three distinct messages which, when applied together, can bring us to a new level of awareness, understanding, and spiritual peace. When the world is not working in the manner we expect or hope, it can affect us physically, emotionally, and spiritually. With an in-depth tarot reading, we can learn to rise above current circumstances to realize the higher purpose of our life experiences, and how they will move us one step closer to personal wholeness and our perfect destiny.

Exploring the Three Faces of the Tarot: Divinatory, Therapeutic, and Spiritual

What information can one access with the tarot? Each card contains three very different messages for us to consider. Primarily, these cards can be used for fortune telling or divination—that is—revealing information about the future. They can also be used for therapeutic healing; to divulge ways in which one can change one's destiny and/or restore emotional well-being. Tarot is also a powerful tool for encouraging spiritual growth and awareness, revealing the higher purpose behind life's challenges.

When you are able to take all three faces of the tarot into consideration during your readings, you will discover a vast treasure of new meanings hidden within the cards. As you grow in skill and understanding, your tarot cards will reveal more and more to you. Whether you are looking for specific answers, greater understanding, or spiritual direction, each card can adapt to your concerns, and provide endless avenues of information for you to consider.

As an example, let's look at the first major arcana card, the Fool. In its most basic interpretation, this card predicts a journey, a fresh start, or a new beginning filled with possibilities. Depending on the querent's focus—business, relationship, or finances—you will want to view the card as it relates to the topic at hand. With each new card you draw, the meaning of the initial card will expand and change. If your second card is the Ten of Swords, it is speaking to a delay or a short circuit in the querent's plans and would in this case change the reading's course. If someone is asking about a new career, these two cards together would indicate blocks to movement; if their question is about a new relationship and its long-term potential, these two cards combined would suggest it may be troubled early on.

Taking these two cards to the next level, the therapeutic message is that the querent will need to look at his or her dreams more closely, to determine what needs to be changed within themselves before their new journey can begin. In the case of a new career, the querent may need to consider higher education, or they could be pursuing a career that is not in their best interest. In a new relationship, the querent should be cautioned to look for red flags and to be true to themselves. If the relationship falls apart in its early stages, it may have something to do with blocks the querent is creating (whether intentionally or not), or the relationship itself simply may not "be in the cards." Armed with this information, it will be easier for the reader to guide the querent's focus back to him or herself. This way, the querent can determine what needs to change before moving forward or how to become empowered, allowing for a different outcome.

Spiritually, the combination of the Fool and the Ten of Swords refers to blocks within oneself. The cards may be asking the querent to examine where he or she feels cut off from Spirit, possibly explaining why attempts at a new beginning continue to fail. Once the querent reestablishes a connection to Spirit, blocks will fall to the wayside and the person can begin pursuing his or her interests once again.

Another example is the Four of Pentacles. In its predictive form, it can indicate holding onto something. One might be building a fortune in a somewhat miserly fashion, jealously keeping information, or physically putting on weight. On an emotional level, this person could be holding onto old ideas, hiding behind self-made walls, or isolating him- or herself.

As a spiritual card, the Four of Pentacles can indicate someone who is cut off from Spirit, one who refuses to share personal gifts with the world, or a person who moves through life feeling fearful or unprotected—a manifestation of being disconnected from the self.

Further on, we will examine how each card expands and adjusts to the querent's questions and the influence of surrounding cards. The reader can then learn how to extract the three meanings of each card to make it speak to any situation or question.

Fate, Destiny, and Free Will

People often attribute life circumstances to fate, destiny, or even karma. Does this suggest that everything in our world is beyond our control? What about the concept of "free will"?

Metaphysically, there will always be events in our lives that are out of our control. How we view fate or destiny holds a direct correlation to our mental, emotional, and spiritual health. If we find ourselves unable to accept or move in tandem with the world around us, we can begin to feel depressed, hopeless, or persecuted on some level. Our ability to trust in the wisdom of the Universe becomes compromised, and we begin to act in ways that promote more "bad luck", or set us up for failure.

Tarot can help us see the bigger picture, along with the higher purpose of what might appear on the surface to be unfortunate events. Most of us can recall a difficult time in our past and acknowledge the gifts and growth that emerged as a result. With the tarot, we can discover beforehand the blessings that will come from our current struggles, making it easier to accept and move through them with greater trust.

Free will suggests that we can change our destiny and our future; in many cases, the tarot can help us create this transformation. During a reading, a querent might discover there will be trouble if they take a certain path such as traveling during a certain time or quitting a job in the hopes that a new one will "magically" appear. The cards may warn against becoming involved with a certain person, or investing money in what appears to be a lucrative enterprise. When these situations arise, the querent will often have a choice to make—this is where the concept of "free will" comes into play.

On a therapeutic level, one might have a history of failed relationships, or be unable to handle money properly. The tarot cards, along with the reader's guidance, can point out certain habits or behaviors that may be contributing to these patterns. The cards themselves can identify the source of these habits, whether they began in a past life, were taught in childhood, or are based in a traumatic cycle the querent is subconsciously repeating. If the querent is ready to break these cycles and embrace free will as a means for change, the tarot cards can offer solid guidance, advice, and specific methods for direction.

Spiritually, the querent may need to release control and turn problems over to the Universe for resolution. But first, the querent must agree to relinquish pre-conceived notions of free will, let go of ego-based desires, and rely on a higher source to correct current difficulties. In this case, the tarot cards offer direct guidance to the querent about how to let go and trust in Spirit to resolve personal struggles.

Visual Literacy

Though it's important to understand the cards' basic meanings, visual literacy plays an important role in learning how to pick up their psychic messages. Depending on the tarot deck you use and the type of reading you perform, becoming visually literate will allow you to delve deeper into the messages specific to your questions. Because the images in each deck can vary, it is essential that you let the symbolic icons of each individual card speak to you.

For example, if you are performing a channeling reading, you might notice a majority of the images drawn contain a common theme such as stars or animals (i.e. the dog who appears on the Fool card, or the lion depicted in the Strength card) that might suggest additional insights to explore. Perhaps the person you are channeling was an astronomer (stars or the Star card), or had a pet you should mention (the Fool, Strength, or Empress cards). Maybe this spirit went on an African safari at some point during his or her lifetime (suggested by the lion depicted in the Strength card). If these images stand out to you, do not hesitate to ask the querent if they carry specific meaning for the loved one you are channeling.

Study the cards for images that speak to you. As you practice this method of reading, you may spot something you have never seen before, activating a new understanding or interpretation of the card.

Once you become visually literate, you will be able to read the cards for any given situation. The tarot can address health issues, help one find a new career, determine the timing of events, or enable one to find lost objects or people. In the appendices, we will explore the endless variations of card meanings singularly and in combination with others, helping you adapt each card's image or theme to the subject or question you are addressing.

The Ever-Evolving Meanings of the Cards

A card's meaning will change and adapt to your readings depending on the focus of your questions and whether it is combined with additional cards. If your question is about health, for instance, card definitions will carry a different tone than if you're asking about romance. In a health-related reading, a card from the suit of cups may indicate the querent needs to drink more water or suggest possible issues involving bodily fluids. For a love reading, these same cards would address emotions (see page 9 for a list of minor arcana associations). As you study the example readings in each chapter, you will begin to see how the cards can always be adapted to the question at hand.

When you perform a reading, the cards' meanings and messages will continue to evolve with every card you draw. Like an unfolding story, the combination of certain cards will bring messages into focus. Perhaps a querent would like to know more about a man she's recently met, and whether he's interested in her romantically. The first card you pull might be the Magician. This could be read as someone who can bring magic into her life or someone very accomplished at whatever he does. However, if the second card is the Devil, this changes the Magician's meaning: these two cards together indicate that this man may be untrustworthy or deceptive. If the third card in the layout is the Three of Cups, a card that typically portrays three women dancing, you might suspect that he is seeing more than one woman at a time. This is important information for your querent to know, especially if she has started to develop serious feelings for him.

On the other hand, let's say that after drawing the Magician, you pull the Ace of Cups and the Ten of Cups. These cards would cast a more positive view on her new boyfriend and the connection, as they indicate the start of a loving and enduring relationship.

You can also look for a specific grouping of cards to appear, affirming the question being asked. For example, a querent might wonder if his or her daughter is pregnant. In this case, the reader would watch for mother-related cards such as the Empress, the Three of Pentacles (an internment or the start of a new experience), the Queen of Pentacles (a female holding a pentacle, representing a baby in her arms, or womb), or the Sun (usually depicting a small child riding atop a horse).

The appendices contain more information on card groupings and combinations, along with additional meanings for each card as they relate to relationships, health, finance, and professions.

A Note on Reversals

Because the tarot contains seventy-eight cards of varied natures, it is not necessary to learn or use the reverse meanings of the cards, that is, cards that appear upside-down in a spread. There are enough images in the deck to cover any question you might ask. As you lay out the cards, if some of them come up reversed, simply turn them right side up and continue with the reading.

Occasionally, you may notice that almost all the cards come up reversed. In general, this can indicate a reversal in the situation you are asking about, though interpreting each individual card is not necessary.

You are welcome to learn reverse tarot card meanings to access more information while you read the cards. However, as a rule, I've found the upright messages of the cards themselves will tell you what you need to know.

Beginner, Intermediate, and Advanced Readings

This book has been divided into three chapters. Because we will be looking at the tarot in a brand new way, the layouts and examples in each chapter provide a step-by-step method that promotes a natural evolution of understanding as you build your reading skills.

The chapter containing the beginner readings will affirm your knowledge about the cards' basic meanings and introduce you to methods that will help you extract other dimensional messages within them. Each reading will take you on a progressive journey through the basics of three-fold interpretation.

As you become comfortable learning to recognize the healing and spiritual aspects of each card, the intermediate chapter will challenge you to look at more complex situations. The chapter on intermediate readings include layouts for general readings, as well as question-specific spreads such as the Relationship and Crossroads readings.

The advanced readings in chapter 3 explore metaphysical topics such as dream interpretation, channeling, and past lives. These readings are designed to help you delve deeper into the mysterious spiritual forces that shape our world.

In addition to the fifteen original layouts presented, the appendices offer a quick reference guide with expanded meanings for the tarot. Here you will find a comprehensive source of information to help you read the tarot with more power and accuracy, including a section on the basic definitions of each card, directions for choosing a significator, and guidelines on how to interpret card combinations. The appendices also offer a section on timing, and a number of spiritual rituals that can help you become more personally empowered using the major arcana cards.

The Tarot Decks in the Sample Readings

For each original layout in this book, three examples are provided to guide the reader through the process of accessing the various dimensions of a reading. I have chosen three different tarot decks for use in these examples. These decks are consistent with traditional tarot, while each offers its own unique illustrations. This will enable you to build your visual literacy by considering the slight variations depicted in each card.

The first sample reading for each layout uses the Lo Scarabeo Tarot deck. This deck combines three traditions of tarot, offering a blend of themes made famous by some of the most influential decks in the history of this divinational art.

The Gilded Tarot is used in the second reading for each layout. This deck carries some of the most striking art available in tarot cards, rich in color and imagery. The Gilded Tarot is easy to interpret and, with its captivating images, will offer you an alternative view of their very traditional meanings.

The Universal Tarot illustrates the third sample reading for each layout. Created through the combined efforts of famous occultist Arthur E. Waite and artist Roberto De Angelis, it is ideal for divination and advanced study, inclusive of all elements of the traditional tarot, combined in new and interesting ways.

Typically, seasoned readers own a number of tarot decks. They will often favor a deck based on a querent's Sun sign, the nature of the question being asked (money, health, romance), or by intuition. This affords the reader the option to choose specific decks to address a variety of issues.

By studying the images, tone, or theme of a tarot deck, you can program it to represent one of the four elements of life, a certain astrological sign, or a particular topic. For instance, the Lo Scarabeo deck used in this book's sample readings carries a lighter tone, so you might choose it to represent the element of air, best used if you are working with an air sign querent (Gemini, Libra, or Aquarius), performing a reading as the sun travels through an air sign month (June, October, or February) or, when the focus of the reading has to do with communication, intellectual pursuits or new ideas.

The Universal deck contains a more grounded energy, ideal for earth sign querents (Taurus, Virgo, or Capricorn), while performing a reading as the sun moves through an earth sign (May, September, or January), or to explore matters of finance, physical health, or material possessions.

The Gilded Tarot carries a softer and more emotional tone, so you might opt for this deck when you read for water signs (Cancer, Scorpio, or Pisces) or during the months connected with this element (July, November, or March). These cards are ideal for questions concerning romance, emotional issues, and family relationships.

You may opt for a deck with vibrant colors or images to use in connection with the element of fire, such as the Witches or Klempt Tarot. These decks can correspond to fire signs (Aries, Leo, or Sagittarius), the months of April, August, and December, and questions regarding creative enterprises, business, and spirituality.

Expanding the Meanings of the Minor Arcana

Traditionally, certain aspects of life are attributed to the four minor arcana suits:

Wands—Spiritual pursuits and business ventures

Cups—Emotions and relationships

Swords—Ideas, communication, and mental health

Pentacles—Finances, material possessions, and physical health

The suits are also assigned to represent the four seasons of the year:

Wands—Spring

Cups—Summer

Swords—Autumn

Pentacles—Winter

Each suit rules a particular element and certain signs of the Zodiac:

Wands—Fire—Aries/Leo/Sagittarius

Cups—Water—Cancer/Scorpio/Pisces

Swords—Air—Gemini/Libra/Aquarius

Pentacles—Earth—Taurus/Virgo/Capricorn

Keep these concepts in mind as you perform a reading. They will help you determine more accurately what dimensions of a situation the cards are addressing and can aid in predicting a timeframe or season in which an event might occur.

While you read, pay close attention to images on the cards, as well as the number of major and minor arcana that appear in a layout. The more major arcana cards you have, the more prominent or important message they are sending.

Also note the numbers or Roman numerals on each card. These numbers can offer clues to time frames, amounts of money, groupings of people, or attempts one may have to make before a goal may be reached. Repetitive numbers often carry important messages, offering more insight as you read. Incorporating numerology into your readings will add another dimension to the cards' messages.

Validating Your Readings

Two of the greatest challenges practitioners of the tarot face are accuracy and validation. For this reason, it is a good idea to watch for confirmation during and after your readings. Being vigilant and receptive will not only add credibility to your tarot practice, it will increase your knowledge base for future readings.

The most reliable source for validation is the querent. Feel free to ask them questions about the cards and reading as it unfolds. Explain to the person that the more communication there is between you two, the more information will be revealed. If you come across a card that neither you nor the querent can validate, make a note to come back to it later. Rest assured that its message will come through as the reading progresses.

Because *Tarot Prediction & Divination* offers a variety of layouts, you can validate answers you receive from one reading by reshuffling, and asking again using an alternate layout. For example, if, after using the Inverted Pyramid to do a reading about a relationship you still have questions or want to validate what you discovered in the reading, you might then use the Relationship or the Yes or No readings for further confirmation.

When asking about a certain person or object, use the significator charts in appendix B to select a card that represents the person or item the querent is asking about. Significator cards play an important role in directing the tarot to a specific person, place, or object. Not only will they help you to focus on the subject at hand, they are a great tool for verifying answers you receive.

Many of the layouts in this book ask for a significator card. When you have located the significator card for your specific reading, place it in the designated position for the layout you are using. This is an ideal way to validate that the cards are addressing the correct person or object.

While performing a reading, you can pull additional cards for any aspect of a situation that remains unclear. For example, if you are doing a health reading and recognize trouble (indicated by a card such as the Tower, Ten of Swords, or other image that suggests a problem is brewing), you can pull more cards from the top of the deck to identify the area or specific issue the querent needs to address. (For more details, consult the section on health, located in appendix C.) Let's say that during a Daily Advice reading you pull the Star card, indicating a wish will come true that day. Pulling a few more cards can offer more information about the event. Any time you want more information, feel free to pull additional cards for clarity or validation.

Keeping a tarot diary can help you validate your predictions, as you will be able to refer back to them to see how accurate they were. As you become more proficient at prediction and divination, this diary will reflect your progress and help you continue to build on the interpretations of the cards.

After a reading, invite the querent to follow up with you at a later date, to verify which predictions came to pass, or to compare how well the reading matched with their experience. Because things do not always happen in a literal sense, you may have to show them how what occurred was actually portrayed in the cards. You do not want to exaggerate the circumstances to force validation, but oftentimes you will be able to see things that the less-than-objective querent will not.

For example, during a general reading I did with a friend, I noticed she was going to receive an unexpected amount of money the following day (indicated by the Four of Cups and Six of Pentacles). Excited at the prospect, and assuming that her father would be the source of the money, she waited anxiously by the mailbox that day. When nothing arrived in the mail, she was quick to let me know that the cards had been wrong. I apologized, but still felt she was going to receive money that day.

A week later, she casually mentioned that a regular monthly check she receives had unexpectedly been placed in her account a few days early (due to an upcoming holiday). I realized that the deposit was made the very day the cards had predicted. Because she decided beforehand how and from whom the money would come, she had not considered that it might appear in an alternate manner, or from a different source.

Occasionally, you may draw a series of cards that appear to make no sense. For instance, if you are inquiring about a financial matter and pull a multitude of cup cards, the reading may be addressing a question your querent has not yet asked. This would be the time to ask your querent if there are any emotional or relationship issues the cards might be addressing. If so, it's just fine to shift your focus to the subject at hand. Once finished, you can reshuffle and ask the original question again.

As you learn to trust the cards to lead you in the right direction, your readings will become more powerful and directed. You will find that your predictions have moved beyond speculation and much closer to validation.

Programming and Personalizing Your Tarot Deck

Once you have familiarized yourself with the general meanings of the cards, you can request that certain cards appear in a reading to indicate an affirmative answer. For example, if your question involves whether or not the querent will relocate to a different city, you might ask that the Knight of Pentacles (whose meaning is physical movement or change) appear in the layout as solid confirmation.

Perhaps your querent wants to know if a certain person is interested in them romantically. You might request of the cards that if the answer is yes, the Lovers or a majority of cup cards appear within the reading.

For most questions, you will be able to locate a card in the deck that contains an image related to the question at hand; when you discover it, you can program it by focusing on the card and asking that it appear somewhere in the layout. Return the card to the deck, shuffle, and begin your reading. For more guidance, consult the card combinations in appendix C to determine which image might best represent an affirmative answer to your question.

If you encounter a card you simply cannot connect with, or one that seems to defy interpretation (for example, the Hierophant or the World), the following two practices can help.

The first method involves sleeping for one night with this card under your pillow. This can evoke new understanding, as you will often find that the image or theme of the card appears in your dreams. (Please do not attempt to learn the entire deck by placing it under your pillow, or you will never get any sleep!)

Another way to increase your understanding of a certain card's meaning is to meditate with it. During the meditation, ask the card to reveal its meaning to you. If you do not receive an answer, study the images and assign your own definition to the card. I had a student who could not come to terms with the basic meanings of the Hierophant card, so she programmed it to mean, "God says . . ." By doing so, she bypassed blocks she had previously encountered when this card appeared in a reading, and now interprets it to mean that the cards to follow it will be a direct message from Spirit.

Reading for Others

Once you become proficient with the cards, you may consider reading professionally, or for friends and family. Here are a few guidelines to make your readings more powerful, effective, and informative.

First, evaluate your querents carefully to determine if they are the type of people who only want to hear good news, or if they prefer that you share everything you see with them. If you are not sure which category they fall into, feel free to ask.

Not everything you sense or see should be shared with querents, so you must read responsibly. Your goal is to guide and empower your querents with information and awareness. Keep this in mind if you spot something that might upset, depress, or frighten them. If something comes up that might cause worry but needs to be addressed, present it to them in the best light possible, using the "forewarned is forearmed" approach. Offer them suggestions on the best way to proceed or how to avoid making a wrong choice altogether. Even in less-than-ideal circumstances, a tarot reading is designed to help someone walk through a challenge with faith, hope, and power. Remember to use the therapeutic and spiritual aspects of the cards to help your querents deal with any challenge you foresee.

Reading for Birth or Death Situations

Predicting pregnancy or death can present a challenge to even the most seasoned tarot reader, so here are a few guidelines to follow when you're asked about these touchy subjects.

If you find yourself uncomfortable with these topics, let your querent know at the beginning of the reading that you do not address health-related subjects. It is perfectly all right to set boundaries around your readings in this manner and is common practice amongst readers and psychic websites to avoid liability issues.

If you are willing to read on health issues, you can also remove the Death and other cards from the deck that make you uncomfortable without compromising the accuracy of your reading. You might do this to keep the client from becoming upset at the sight of negative cards that could lead them to incorrect or upsetting conclusions.

Many readers are open to reading on the subjects of health, pregnancy, illness, and death. The most important thing to remember as you address these issues is that as a tarot reader, your job is to empower the querent, no matter what revelations appear in the reading. If you see trouble coming in any of the aforementioned subject areas, you can alert your querent to practice more caution and awareness, seek medical help, or prepare for the spiritual challenge of a change in current situations.

For example, a client may want to know if or when she will become pregnant. Typically, this is a question filled with hope and expectancy. If the reading reveals a physical reason she has not become pregnant, you can advise her to seek information from a fertility specialist. The cards may also reveal that it is not time for her to become pregnant, but that she will conceive at some time in the future.

If a querent is pregnant and asks for a reading on how the pregnancy will go, again—read with caution. If Death or the Three of Swords appears, this could indicate a miscarriage or stillbirth. This is not news you want to give to an unsuspecting client, so before you read on this type of subject, you may want to remove cards of this nature from the deck if you are performing the reading in person.

In 99 percent of cases in which the Death card appears in a layout, it is predicting transformation on a spiritual or emotional level, **not** a physical demise. If you sense a physical death coming, unless the querent has asked specifically, I recommend keeping this information to yourself. You will not be helping the querent if you reveal something that could be this upsetting.

If a querent asks specifically about the impending death of a loved one, such as parents or spouses who are on life support or obviously near the end of their lives, they are inquiring about time frames. In this situation they are already preparing for a loved one to cross over, so the information you share with them will carry a different tone. If you feel querents in this situation are prepared to hear the truth, you can advise them openly.

As a general rule, practice caution when reading on these subjects. If you feel uneasy addressing these issues, it is best to advise a querent that you are unable to do readings about these topics.

During your tarot readings, invite querents to be interactive in the process. Do not hesitate to have them verify what you sense or to clarify any cards that in essence, could address more than one topic. When you work together as a team, you can offer greater guidance in faster and more comprehensive ways. (I often encourage my querents to "think of me as a doctor and tell me where it hurts." That way, I can get down to the business of enlightening them more quickly.)

As you read for others, it is often helpful to address them in the language of their zodiac sign. When I perform a reading, I always ask querents their birthdate. Knowing querents' signs and the associated elements will enable you to advise them in a most effective manner.

When reading for water signs, (Cancer, Scorpio, or Pisces), you'll want to use words that correspond with emotion. For example, "I feel that . . ." or "I am sensing . . ." as openers to deliver your message. For air signs who thrive on thought and communication, (Gemini, Libra, or Aquarius), use phrases such as "I think that . . ." or "The cards are telling me . . ."

The fire signs (Aries, Leo, and Sagittarius) respond to inspirational or passionate approaches. Begin your predictions with lines such as "I'm excited to tell you that . . ." or "What you are going to need to do is . . ." A Taurus, Virgo, or Capricorn (the earth signs) will listen for tangible and practical direction, responding to such phrases as "I see here that . . ." or "The cards are showing me . . ."

Your querents will be very interested in the images on the cards and want to know what they mean. As they view the images and scan them for signs of affirmation, your querents will become more open and interactive during the reading. Take the time to point out any images or objects on the cards that confirm the predictions you make. For example, point out when a high number of pentacle cards appear in a money reading, or when cup cards dominate the layout in a relationship reading. Offering the querent insight into how you extract information from each card will not only increase their trust in you; it will strengthen their belief in the power of the tarot itself.

Based on a fear of encountering the Devil, Death, or other upsetting card, some people hesitate to have a tarot reading. You may be unsure of how to read these cards yourself, or how to assure your querent that the cards' meanings are usually not literal. There is an easy solution to this dilemma: remove any cards that you feel would cast a negative or upsetting tone to your readings. Removing certain key cards from your tarot deck will not limit or alter the effectiveness of your readings. In fact, when you don't have to worry about these cards appearing and frightening querents, you'll be able to advise them with greater confidence.

In the event that you are unable to answer a querent's question or the cards appear vague, resist the urge to make something up on the spot. You can attempt to address the question with an alternate layout, or simply tell the querent that the cards are not able to divulge specific information about their question at this time.

Above all, remember that your job as a reader is to uplift, advise, and empower your querent so they can move forward in a positive way. It is not your responsibility to make other peoples' decisions for them; your role as a tarot reader is to provide enlightenment about available options, predict the future outcome of a choice or event, and reveal hidden aspects of a situation that provide querents with enough information to help them make the most empowered choices for themselves.

Additional Uses for the Tarot

The diversity of the tarot extends far beyond the art of divination. You can use the major arcana cards in the deck to improve your meditation skills, access healing abilities, and empower your thoughts, actions, and spiritual awareness.

The empowerment guide in appendix E encourages you to explore the numerous ways in which you can improve your life using the major arcana cards. This section offers a variety of exercises and rituals, and includes a major arcana empowerment chart for use with gemstone, color, and aromatherapy techniques and applications.

One

BEGINNER READINGS

YES OR NO READING

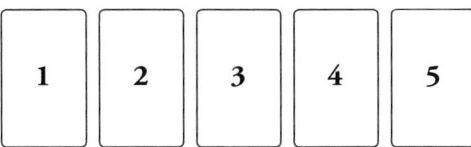

The Yes or No Reading is ideal for beginners or for those who would like a quick and simple answer to a question. If you are new to the tarot, this layout will provide you with an initial sense of how the cards can speak directly to your concerns.

Once you obtain the answer to your question, it is helpful to look a bit deeper by reading the message of each card. If you are a beginner, this is an excellent way to learn basic meanings. When you explore each image individually and consider its relation to surrounding cards, you will discover additional information about the situation.

Directions: Shuffle the cards as you concentrate on your yes/no question. Then draw the first five cards from the top of the pile and lay them out left to right, as illustrated.

Use the following key to read the cards:

Major arcana = Yes (considered "even")
Court cards = No (considered "odd") (kings, queens, knights, pages, or knaves)
Minor arcana:
  Even Number = Yes
  Odd Number = No

As an example, let's say that the following cards were drawn for a question:

Seven of Wands (NO)
Two of Swords (YES)

Two of Clubs (YES)
Hanged Man (YES)
Strength (YES)

With two major arcana and two minor arcana "yes" cards in the layout, we would consider this a clear affirmative response.

The stronger the influence of the cards in a layout, the stronger the answer you will receive. For example, a predominance of major arcana cards would be a confident "yes", while four or five court cards would be a definite "no".

A mix of major and minor arcana and court cards will provide a definitive answer if four of them indicate a "yes" or a "no." When you come across two and three combinations (for instance two major arcana and three court cards, or three odd and two even numbered cards of the minor arcana), you may want to investigate further until you feel confident with the answer you receive.

When you pull all even cards for a "yes" answer, or all odd cards for a "no" answer, you can feel confident about the message they are sending.

After you determine the answer to your questions, study each card individually to access additional information and messages the cards are sending.

(Original concept/design by Louise Gilbertson)

Brad's Career Advancement Reading

Brad is currently employed but searching for a new job. He wanted to know, "Will I get the job I just interviewed for?"

The five cards he drew in response were:

> Four of Cups
> Two of Swords
> Justice
> The Hanged Man
> Nine of Pentacles

Based on the two even minor and two major arcana cards pulled, the answer is a resounding "yes." The Nine of Pentacles is a "no" card, but is the only one in this layout.

Looking at the cards from a predictive angle, we can see the process Brad will go through before his "yes" answer comes true. The Four of Cups in the first position indicates a job that came to his attention in an unexpected way, rather than through want ads or online listings. This card typically represents boredom, followed by an invitation or gift that appears out of the blue.

The Two of Swords indicates a time of indecision, so it could be a while before the company decides who to hire. Because of this, Brad may not hear anything for a few weeks (the Two of Swords indicating a timeframe as well as a stage of the process). The Justice card affirms that efforts Brad put into submitting his résumé and attending the interview will pay off, while the Hanged Man implies a second period of waiting before he hears about the job. The Nine of Pentacles, as the final card, represents a positive and abundant outcome.

Emotionally, the Four of Pentacles addresses Brad's desire to move out of a rut and into new challenges, as well as a drive to experience more fulfillment and success in his career. The Two of Swords hints that he may be unsure of how to move forward and leave the job he currently has. The Justice card reminds him to trust in the fairness of the Universe, in turn promising that efforts to move into a new position will pay off. During this process he will experience a time of waiting, as indicated by the

Yes or No Reading
Brad's Career Advancement

Hanged Man. This will give him time to process and move through any doubts or fears he may have about his chances of getting the new job. The Nine of Pentacles represents the new level of abundance and security that will emerge from his efforts.

Spiritually, these cards as a whole are asking him to trust in the process, follow his intuition (the Four of Cups, which displays a figure looking up to heaven for answers), and to sit in the unknown for a time (Two of Swords, the Hanged Man). Once he has completed the footwork, it is important that Brad trust in the Universe, and leave the results up to it (Justice). The Hanged Man indicates the need to go inward to manifest this new job, and to remain focused on spirit, faith, and destiny. The Nine of Pentacles affirms that Brad will experience many spiritual rewards for his willingness to take this leap of faith.

Debbie's Business Investment Reading

Debbie is considering forming a partnership with her brother, and asked, "Should I invest in my brother Keaton's new business venture?"

The five cards she drew in response were:

> Ace of Cups
> Page/Knave of Wands
> Queen of Pentacles
> The Devil
> Ace of Swords

Four of the five cards drawn in this reading are "no" cards; the only "yes" card is the Devil. These cards clearly indicate that investing in her brother Keaton's business would be a bad idea.

Taking the cards at face value, the Ace of Cups (Aces representing new ideas and beginnings) and the Page/Knave of Wands (pages/knaves meaning messages or proposals) affirm that Debbie's brother has approached her about investing in his business. The Queen of Pentacles represents Debbie, portraying her as someone who has money to lend or invest. The appearance of the Devil indicates Debbie's hesitation to immerse herself in this business, while the Ace of Swords recommends she request more information, or express her misgivings to Keaton. The Ace of Swords also serves as a card that warns Debbie to protect herself.

Emotionally, Debbie loves her brother and wants to support him, as indicated by the Ace of Cups. She may also feel that his idea is inspired, shown by the Page of Wands, but senses that Keaton is depending on her finances (Queen of Pentacles) to get this idea off the ground. This kind of dependency could make her feel uneasy, or fill her with guilt if she decides not to help him (represented by the Devil). The Ace of Swords may speak to her reluctance to turn the offer down, even though this reading indicates that it is in her best interest to do so.

Spiritually, the Universe is giving Debbie the opportunity to examine this situation from a deeper place. Refusing to invest in Keaton's business doesn't mean that Debbie doesn't love her brother (Ace of Cups). It simply means she must trust her

Yes or No Reading
Debbie's Business Investment

intuition (Page of Wands) and pay attention to what it is telling her. Even though she has the money to invest (Queen of Pentacles), she senses it would be a costly move for her (the Devil). The Ace of Swords reminds Debbie that she will need to put herself first, turn down Keaton's offer and protect her assets, as Spirit is directing her.

Heather's Relationship Reading

Heather is concerned about her love relationship and asked, "Is my partner being faithful to me?"

The five cards she drew were:

> The Tower
> Eight of Swords
> Ten of Pentacles
> Knight of Wands
> Five of Cups

In this reading we have three "yes" cards and two "no" cards. The answer is favorable, but because the message of The Tower typically implies an upset of some kind, we should look a little deeper into the situation. Though we can assume that Heather's partner is being faithful, the cards as a whole indicate trouble somewhere in the relationship.

The Tower reveals that there has been a recent upset in the partnership, while the Eight of Swords suggests Heather's inability to see or think clearly about the relationship (indicated by the blindfold in this image). Often, when couples are having difficulties, one or both partners may suspect that a third person outside the relationship is creating the problem, hence Heather's question regarding her boyfriend's faithfulness. The Ten of Pentacles indicates that there is a strong foundation in this relationship, but that it is being undermined by anger, resentment, or self-centered behavior, portrayed by the Knight of Wands. The Five of Cups indicates emotional fear or sorrow, born out of Heather's perception of the situation.

Emotionally, Heather is questioning the relationship and her partner's loyalty, indicating that she has some work to do. She is looking outside herself for the cause of her unhappiness, when in truth, the answers lie within. Frequent arguments, as represented by the Tower, as well as the Knight of Wands, can indicate that one or both parties carry grudges or expectations that are not being met. These emotions are usually based in fear or lack of understanding, and often indicate that one or both parties are neither being true to themselves, nor honest with their partner

Yes or No Reading
Heather's Relationship

about how they feel. The Eight of Swords suggests that Heather could be stuck in old thought patterns or reliving past experiences, and is unable to look beyond herself to consider the facts. She is ignoring or perhaps unaware of the truth that something within her needs to change. The Ten of Pentacles is a card that encourages her to look at things more realistically, review the facts, and pay more attention to the positive aspects of this connection. With the Five of Cups in the last position, Heather may need counseling or outside guidance to break a pattern of fear or disappointment, most likely rooted in her past.

Spiritually, these cards reveal the inner turmoil that is creating external problems in their relationship. The Tower suggests the need for a cleansing and clearing of negative thought patterns (represented by the Eight of Swords). The Ten of Pentacles indicates that Heather is focused on eliciting outside affirmation from her partner, and needs to work on strengthening her own spiritual confidence (indicated by the Knight of Wands). The Five of Cups represents the need to grieve and release the past. Note that both the first and last cards in this reading suggest that spiritual cleansing and emotional healing will be key in Heather's ability to resolve her fears surrounding this relationship.

DAILY ADVICE READING

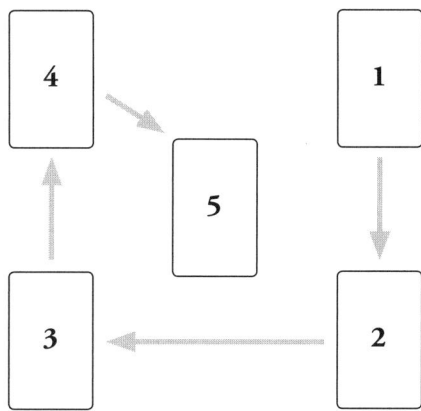

Laying out a few cards each day for direction or advice of a general nature is good practice for those who are learning the meanings and symbolism of the tarot, as well as for seasoned readers who would like an overview of what a particular day might hold. Rather than asking a specific question, you are simply requesting that the tarot cards present you with an overview of the next twenty-four hours.

This reading is helpful if you are facing an important event on a certain day, for example, a job interview, loan approval, or a desire to hear from that special someone. Though you are not asking these questions directly, the cards will reveal if there is potential for these events to occur.

Directions: Shuffle the cards while asking the following question, "What can I know to be true about this day?" Drawing the first five cards from the top of the deck, arrange them in the order shown in the illustration. Read them as you would a clock, keeping in mind that each card will correspond to a certain segment of your day.

You may either leave the cards out to review later in the day or record them in your daily tarot journal. At the end of the day, revisit the cards to see how each one matched up with your actual experiences. Pay close attention to placement, as the events and energy they predict generally happen in sequence.

Jenna's 9/11 Reading

In my beginner's tarot classes, I recommend pulling five cards each morning while asking the question, "What can I know to be true about this day?" In a class I began on a Monday night, I instructed my students to do this, and invited them to call me if they had any questions. At 7:30 the next morning, my phone rang: Jenna was on the other end. She told me that she had pulled her cards for the day and was "freaking out," as she put it.

The five cards she pulled were:

> The World
> The Tower
> Eight of Wands
> The Hanged Man
> Five of Cups

When I asked Jenna why the cards upset her, she told me to turn on my television. Of course, it was September 11, 2001. The cards could not have been clearer or more accurate in their message. The World and the Tower cards literally spelled out the "World Trade Center Towers." The Eight of Wands, a card that indicates air travel, planes, or something coming in quickly, told the rest of the story. These first three cards indicated an event that would unfold in the first half of the day. The Hanged Man predicted that everything would come to a halt and remain in limbo for the rest of the day, and the Five of Cups in the center of the layout spoke to a day filled with sorrow.

Emotionally, the cards predicted that the entire world (the World) would be deeply affected by this sudden and unexpected upset (the Tower), instantly and profoundly (the Eight of Wands). Not only would it alert us to how vulnerable we were from terrorist attacks, it would stop everyone in their tracks (the Hanged Man) and fill them with sorrow and shock (Five of Cups).

Spiritually, a new global awareness (the World) has risen from this tragedy. Because of the many lives lost on that day, each of us would come to contemplate the fragility of life, and the way in which the Universe can change our perceptions in

Daily Advice Reading
Jenna's 9/11 Reading

an instant (the Tower). The Eight of Wands (wands represent spirituality and business) predicted a rapid change in not only our awareness, but the manner in which we travel, and our need to turn to Spirit in all things. When tragedy strikes and we realize how powerless we are, there is often a mass return to religious and spiritual practices. The Hanged Man represented a time of spiritual transformation, inner seeking and soul searching, confirmed by the Five of Cups, a card that predicts a need to release the old or to grieve during a time of loss. These cards confirm that we grow closer to Spirit during times of great despair.

A Day in the Life of the Author Reading

One morning I awoke on a day I had decided to take off work, faced with a somewhat random schedule. I chose to perform a Daily Advice reading to get a glimpse of how the day might unfold.

After asking, "What can I know to be true about this day?" I pulled the following cards:

> Three of Cups
> Seven of Wands
> Page/Knave of Pentacles
> Five of Cups
> Two of Cups

That night I returned to the cards to see how well they matched the events of my day. I had plans to meet with a friend for coffee first thing in the morning. The Three of Cups indicates a celebration or gathering of friends, so it predicted this event accurately. Later, to maintain my commitment to take the day off, I turned down a request from a client, as predicted by the Seven of Wands in position two, which represents defending ones self or position. In the afternoon I received a check in the mail (Page/Knave of Pentacles indicating a message, often regarding money) I had been waiting for. Later that afternoon I spent some time in meditation to release an emotional situation that was nagging at me (Five of Cups). I had no plans for the evening, but, out of the blue, a friend called and invited me to dinner (Two of Cups).

Reviewing the overall layout, this reading contained three cards from the suit of cups. This suggests an easy-going and fulfilling day. The Three of Cups correctly predicted the fun I would have visiting with a friend, while the Seven of Wands alerted me that I might have to say no to someone to maintain my boundaries. The Page/Knave of Pentacles hinted that money I had been waiting for would arrive, which allowed me to relax and attend to my day without financial concern. The Five of Cups alerted me to some emotional sadness that I needed to address, while the Two of Cups predicted an invitation of a positive nature later in the day. As the central card of the layout, it also confirmed a relaxing, joyful, and balanced day.

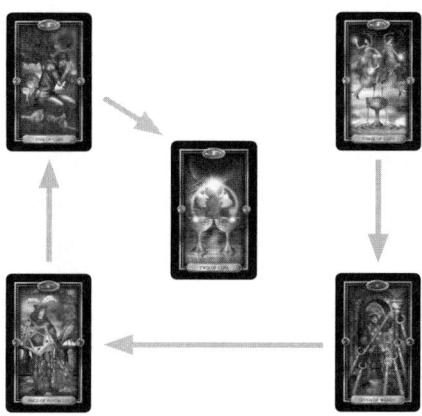

Daily Advice Reading
A Day in the Life of the Author

These cards predicted a spiritually-refreshing period. I communed with friends at both the start and end of my day, (Three of Cups, Two of Cups) which restored my inner sense of well-being. I was also able to stand my ground and be true to myself, another gift of Spirit (Seven of Wands). The cards also predicted that there would be an opportunity to cleanse and release sorrow from the past (Five of Cups), allowing me to move with more spiritual freedom and joy throughout the remainder of the day.

Terry's Daily Advice Reading

Terry was waiting to hear about a number of opportunities—one involving a job interview and another concerning apartment availability in a complex she was hoping to move into. She was also concerned about when she might hear from her current love interest, with whom she had not interacted for a few days. Rather than ask a series of questions, she chose to use the daily advice reading to see what, if anything, might happen in these areas.

The cards she drew were:

> Page/Knave of Pentacles
> Death
> Three of Wands
> Four of Wands
> Ten of Cups

First thing in the morning, Terry received an e-mail (Page/Knave of Pentacles) informing her that she had not gotten the job for which she had interviewed (Death). She decided to let the matter of work rest for a few hours, waiting to see what she should do next. (Note that the suit of pentacles refers to the physical world and finances, and the Three of Wands can refer to work, i.e., in this particular reading, her job.) Later that afternoon, Terry devoted some time to reviewing her resume to make sure its foundation was solid (Four of Wands), and to consider what other jobs might be available in her field. The Four of Wands could also refer to the apartment she was waiting to hear about, as it can represent a home or residence. Because she did not hear anything about the apartment this day, we can assume that the Four of Wands referred to her job search. Her day ended with an affirming conversation with her love interest, as predicted by the Ten of Cups.

Emotionally, the Page/Knave of Pentacles and the Death cards closed the door to the job Terry had interviewed for. On the other hand, it encouraged her to seek a higher perspective (Three of Wands), and to see what she could change to improve her chances next time around (Four of Wands). Though Terry had a disappointing morning, it ended with a joyous interaction that balanced her emotions when she heard from her love interest (Ten of Cups).

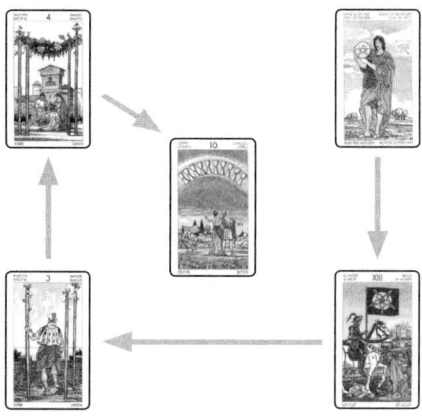

Daily Advice Reading
Terry's Daily Advice

Spiritually, Terry received intuitive direction at each turn of her day. One door closed (Page/Knave of Pentacles and Death) when she was turned down for the job, but, when she returned her focus to Spirit and requested guidance (Three of Wands), she was shown how to move forward. Terry was encouraged to continue her quest for a better job, but this time, with a more stable foundation (Four of Wands). Even though she did not get the job, nor did she hear about the apartment, her love interest came through for her, restoring her spirit and hopes for the future of her romance (Ten of Cups). Trusting in the process and following the direction she received enabled her to move through the day calmly, trusting in the Universe's protection.

THE ILLUMINATING STAR READING

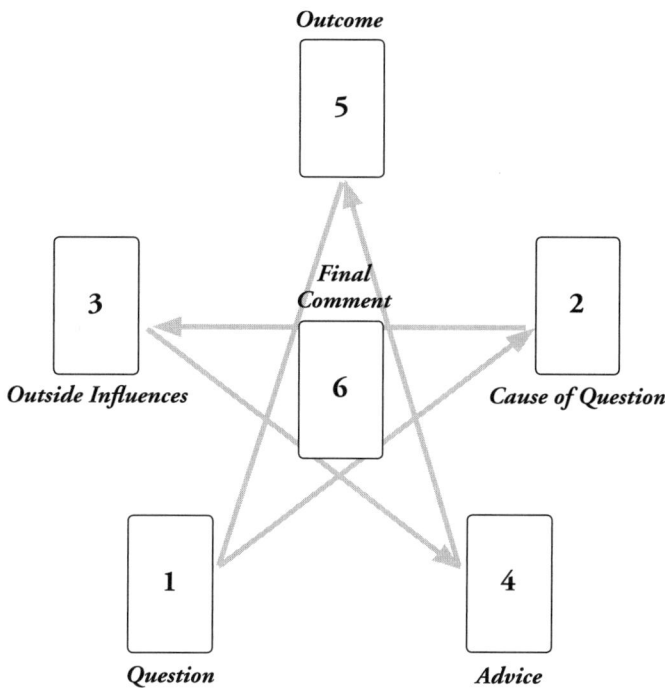

The Illuminating Star reading is ideal for obtaining the answer to a single question or situation, and can bring to light new information or influences of which you might not be aware. In this reading, the position in which a card lands is as important as the card itself. When you consider that each position directs you in a certain way, this will deepen the meaning of the card.

Directions: Concentrate on your question as you shuffle. Then lay the cards out in a star-shaped pattern as shown in the illustrations. Use the following key of the card positions to direct the course of the reading.

Card 1—Defines or confirms the question that you are asking

Card 2—Outlines underlying motives or circumstances that prompted the question

Card 3—Defines outside influences that must be considered in this situation

Card 4—Offers advice for the querent or reader

Card 5—Reveals the outcome or answer to the question

Card 6—Adds a final comment or directive to the reading

Franni's Pet Reading

In this reading, Franni needed to know if she should take her dog to the veterinarian. He had been acting listless, and had not eaten for a few days. She could not determine if he was simply under the weather or if something more serious was going on.

These were the six cards she drew in response:

> The Fool
> Seven of Pentacles
> The Devil
> Knight of Wands
> The Hierophant
> Four of Wands

The first card in this reading represents the question being asked. Notice that The Fool card contains an image of a dog, confirming that this reading is focused on Franni's pet. The Seven of Pentacles (laborious work and effort) verifies the reason for the question. In this case, the concept of "labor" comes into play. Franni has noticed that her dog is moving in labored ways, and has slowed down. In many tarot decks, the person depicted in this card appears to be tired or weary, affirming that the signs Franni is noticing could be cause for concern.

The Devil appears in the outside influence position, indicating a possible hidden cause for her dog's behavior, which needs to be investigated. He may have eaten something that did not agree with him, or there may be bigger problems looming. Knights in the tarot are action cards, so the Knight of Wands in the advice position is a call for Franni to take immediate action.

The Hierophant represents a professional. In the outcome position, this verifies that a visit to the veterinarian is in order. The final comment card, the Four of Wands, indicates that the dog is in reasonably good health, and that whatever is causing the problem can be taken care of by the veterinarian. (Note that if the final comment card had contained a sword card, it might have indicated surgery.)

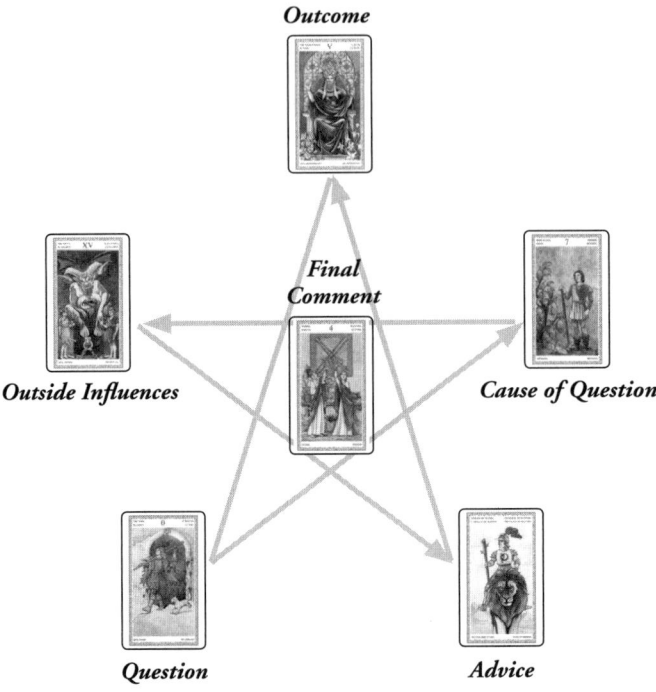

The Illuminating Star Reading
Franni's Pet

Emotionally, the Fool card indicates that Franni has never observed this type of behavior in her dog before. Considering the number of symptoms she has noticed (Seven of Pentacles), she is fearful that something is not right (the Devil). The Knight of Wands indicates that Franni needs to take action. Even if nothing is seriously wrong, she will feel better if she has a professional check on her dog (the Hierophant). Once she does, Franni's sense that everything is all right will return (Four of Wands), and she can release her fears and concerns.

Spiritually, the Fool indicates that her dog's unusual behavior affected Franni's awareness. When trouble appears unexpectedly, as humans, we tend to focus all our attention on the problem and how to resolve it. This is Spirit's way of creating a greater awakening in us, and also gives the Universe a chance to "rearrange the furniture" in other areas of our lives while our attention is on more pressing matters.

The Seven of Pentacles speaks to how invested Franni is in her dog. He has been a companion of hers for quite some time, and they are devoted to each other. Spiritually, the Devil can represent someone who is paralyzed by fear and unsure of which direction to turn. This card is not always an indicator of evil or terrible troubles, but it addresses the idea that we can be undermined by fear or lack of faith. The Knight of Wands is asking Franni to trust the veterinarian (the Hierophant) to determine what action to take, rather than relying on herself to resolve a problem she cannot identify. The Four of Wands promises a return to her normal routine once Franni has passed through this growth-filled and spiritually transforming challenge.

Nathaniel's Crush Reading

In this reading, Nathaniel wanted to know if he should ask out a girl he was interested in. Though there had been some flirtations, he was not sure if she was open to the idea of going on a date with him.

Nathaniel pulled these six cards in response:

>Ace of Swords
>Page/Knave of Swords
>Ace of Cups
>Queen of Cups
>The Sun
>Six of Cups

What is most obvious in this reading is that the suits of swords and cups dominate the layout. Cups represent emotional issues, while swords indicate that, to communicate his interest in this girl, Nathaniel will have to make the first move.

The Ace of Swords in position 1 reflects Nathaniel's desire to ask this girl out, affirming that the cards are addressing his specific question. The reason he is asking this question is to find out if his invitation will be well received. The Page/Knave of Swords, in the number two position, encourages him to move forward, as pages/knaves represent communication of some kind. The card in position 3 speaks to outside influences. In this case, the Ace of Cups indicates that this girl is interested in Nathaniel, and, in fact, has been waiting for him to approach her. (Aces represent a new beginning, and cups represent emotions or romance.)

In the advice position we find the Queen of Cups, a card that represents the girl herself. Not only does this card reveal that she has feelings for him, it also offers Nathaniel advice on the best way to approach her. Residing in the suit of cups, this queen is very feminine, sensitive, and romantically inclined. She may be a bit old-fashioned, which is why she will wait for Nathaniel to ask her out. He can make great headway if he shows up with flowers or a gift, and treats her like a "queen."

The Sun, representing prosperity and loving relationships, resides in the outcome position. As the only major arcana card in this reading, it has a bit more influence

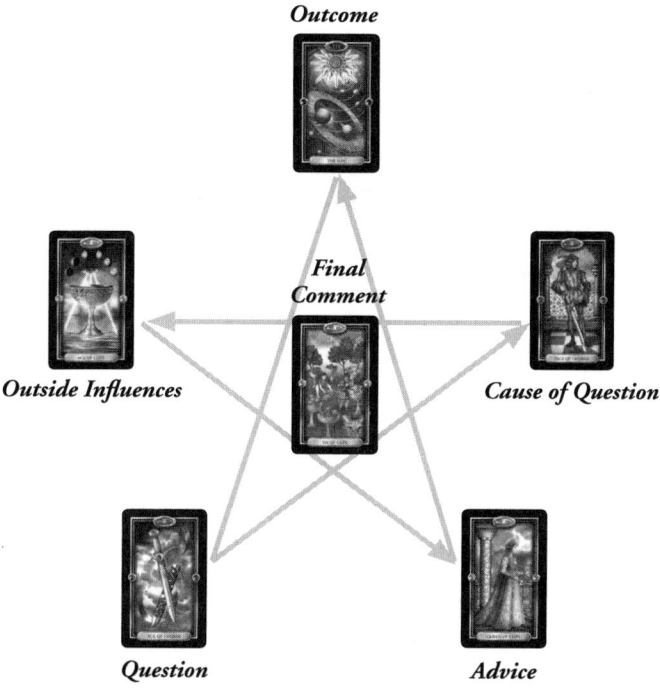

The Illuminating Star Reading
Nathaniel's Crush

than the other cards, and indicates a positive outcome. The Six of Cups, as the final comment card, implies that they will have fun together, and that the relationship has the potential to grow deeper. The Six of Cups is one of the strongest love cards in the minor arcana, and can also indicate past-life or soul-mate connections.

Emotionally, Nathaniel may be hesitant to ask out this girl unless he can be certain of a positive outcome. The Ace and Page of Swords indicate that he has given this matter much thought. The cups in this reading reveal Nathaniel's emotional attachment to a positive outcome. He is very wrapped up in his hopes at this point, and could feel emotionally crushed if she refuses the invitation. However, because the cards in this reading are all positive, I encouraged Nathaniel to trust his instincts and take a chance by asking her out. I also pointed out that until he does, nothing will move forward.

Spiritually, Nathaniel is stuck and is living in his head. The first two cards in the reading are swords, both of which indicate that some mental gymnastics are going on here. These are blocking Nathaniel's ability to trust and follow his heart, indicating a disconnection from himself. If he can release his expectations and simply honor his intuition, he cannot lose. Even if the girl turns him down, this experience will be vital to Nathaniel's personal growth, as he learns to move with spiritual intuition and leave the outcome up to the Universe.

Tom's Job Search Reading

Tom wanted to know when he might find a new job. He is currently unemployed and has been searching diligently for over a year, submitting resumes and going on interviews, with no success. He wants to know when his efforts will pay off, or if he is wasting his time.

He drew these six cards in response:

> Knight of Swords
> Page/Knave of Swords
> Two of Wands
> The Magician
> King of Pentacles
> Seven of Pentacles

The first card defines or confirms Tom's question. Here we have the Knight of Swords, a card that affirms that, for quite some time, he has been putting great effort into his search and sending out feelers. Card 2 reveals the motive behind his search for work. In this case, based on the image in this card, the Page/Knave of Swords could indicate that Tom was let go (or "cut") from his last job. In the number 3 position we have the Two of Wands, a strong indicator that a job offer may be coming his way soon. The suit of wands covers business and spiritual activities, while number 2 cards in a tarot deck usually indicate a proposal or invitation of some kind.

Position 4 offers advice for Tom to consider. In this reading, the number 4 card is the Magician. This card encourages Tom to continue his search and to keep the focus on all the gifts and talents he has to offer.

The King of Pentacles sits in position 5 at the top of the Illuminating Star layout. This king represents wealth, stability, security, and money. In this reading, it promises a stable, long-term job with financial gain. This card indicates that, indeed, Tom's efforts will pay off and a new job will soon come his way.

The final comment card is the Seven of Pentacles. Traditionally, this card refers to "the fruits of one's labor" or "reaping what one sows." As the last card in this

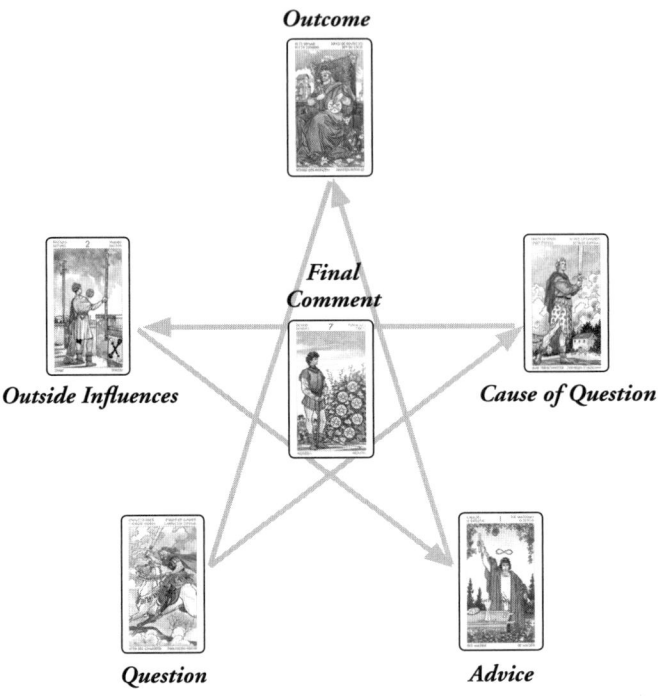

The Illuminating Star Reading
Tom's Job Search

reading, we are assured that whatever effort Tom puts into his quest, the outcome will be worth it.

Emotionally, the Knight of Swords reflects Tom's frustration that nothing seems to be moving forward. The Page/Knave of Swords asks him to stop and listen. It also alerts him not to get caught up in his thoughts or sabotage his efforts with negative thinking. The Two of Wands suggests that Tom remain hopeful and optimistic, trusting that, at some point, the blocks will fall to the wayside. As if by magic, he will come across his ideal job when the time is right, as inferred by the Magician. The King of Pentacles reminds Tom to remain balanced, steady, and determined. The Seven of Pentacles speaks to the emotional abundance and satisfaction that awaits him, once his journey is complete.

Spiritually, Tom's drive for a new job is strong (Knight of Swords). Guidance will come through Spirit if Tom asks, as represented by the Page/Knave of Swords and the Two of Wands. (Notice that the men in both cards are looking up to the heavens.) The Magician refers to Tom's spiritual power, as one who has mastered the elements and is ready to take on something more challenging and fulfilling. Tom is depending on this new job to bring him the physical stability and security he deserves. Spiritually, it speaks to his readiness to move forward into new experiences. The Seven of Pentacles reflects the universal law that no effort is wasted, and no act goes unrewarded.

THE REASONS READING

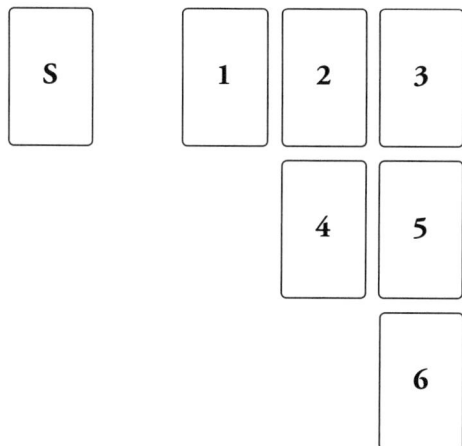

The Reasons reading is designed to help you gain greater insight into someone's motives, or the reasons behind unexpected behavior on another's part. It can answer questions about why something has or has not happened, or why someone is doing, or, in some cases, not doing, what we would like them to. This layout involves using a significator card (see significator tables in appendix B).

Directions: First, consult the significator tables to locate a card that best represents the person or event you are asking about, and place it in the position marked "S" in the layout illustration.

Concentrate on your question while you shuffle the cards, and then lay them out in an asymmetrical pyramid pattern, as shown in the illustrations. Read the cards in each row as a unit, paying close attention to the relationship between the cards, how they affect each other, and their overall message regarding your question.

Cards 1, 2, and 3 will represent what appear to be the reasons for a person's behavior, or the querent's assumption about what is happening.

Cards 4 and 5 will represent anything going on behind the scenes which the querent may be unaware of. This row will give you some new thoughts to consider or reveal hidden influences affecting the situation.

Card 6 will represent the actual reason for the person's behavior, or account for the ways in which events have unfolded. This card will help you understand why someone is not behaving or something is not progressing in the manner anticipated.

Cassie's Financial Reading

Cassie wanted to know, "Why do I continue to have financial woes, despite my best efforts?" She chose the Ace of Pentacles as a significator card because it represents the new (ace) financial balance (pentacles) she hopes to attain.

After shuffling, Cassie drew the following cards:

> Significator—Ace of Pentacles
> Queen of Wands
> Ace of Cups
> Three of Pentacles
> Five of Wands
> Page of Cups
> Death

The first row of this reading represents what Cassie perceives to be her valiant efforts to bring her finances into balance. The Queen of Wands suggests she is practicing higher awareness and fiscal responsibility (two traits associated with this queen in particular). The Ace of Cups implies that she is attempting to practice new emotional awareness. However, it could also refer to the fact that when extra money comes in, it "spills over" (as shown in the image), and gives her a false sense of abundance that encourages her to spend this money immediately. The Three of Pentacles reflects the fact that she is trying to put new practices into effect. This card represents Cassie's efforts to try something new. It also validates her belief that she has been attempting to resolve this problem.

Row two reveals some hidden reasons behind Cassie's inability to restore balance to her finances. She is used to spending money whenever the mood strikes her, (represented by the Page/Knave of Cups), and the Five of Wands indicates that her new budget is creating struggles or conflict within her. When something "calls" to Cassie emotionally, she has trouble resisting the urge to buy it.

The Death card occupies the final position and reveals the true reason she cannot restore balance. Because Cassie has not given up the thoughts or habits that initially created this trouble, her efforts will continue to fail until she experiences a rebirth in thought, feeling, and action toward money.

The Reasons Reading
Cassie's Financial Reading

Emotionally, Cassie continues to handle money in ways that undermine her efforts. She carries an expectation of abundance, represented by the queen, and feels that she deserves to have nice things. The Ace of Cups reveals that she shops to feel better about herself, and that new things brighten her spirits. The idea of being able to restore financial balance makes her feel optimistic (as represented by the Three of Pentacles), but she has not yet learned to follow through.

To resolve this problem, Cassie will have to address her spending habits spiritually. Her need to affirm her own worth (the Queen of Wands) must be replaced with self-love (Ace of Cups). Once she can validate herself spiritually, she can start to build a new foundation and framework for financial balance (Three of Pentacles). She will need to examine the emotional reasons behind her spending (Five of Wands) and replace this addiction with loving messages and affirmations (Page of Cups). Through this process she will experience a spiritual rebirth, the most valid definition of the Death card. To end her financial troubles, she will have to examine and release the past through spiritual means, construct a new belief system, and approach her financial troubles in a more structured way.

Brittany's Marriage Reading

In this reading, Brittany wants to know why her husband has recently become distant. She is feeling confused and worried, and wants to know why he has suddenly changed his behavior. Her husband, Matt, is a Taurus, so Brittany selected the King of Pentacles as the significator card, which represents earth sign men.

She pulled the following cards:

> Significator—King of Pentacles
> Page/Knave of Swords
> Two of Swords
> Four of Swords
> Six of Wands
> Knight of Swords
> The Tower

Note that there is a predominance of swords in this reading. Swords represent thought, communication, and ideas. There is a chance that Brittany's concerns are mostly in her imagination, or that she is taking things too personally.

In the first row, the Page/Knave of Swords indicates that Brittany realizes something is amiss. The lack of communication and affection between her and her husband has alerted her that there is trouble. The Two of Swords implies indecision or lack of clarity, and, in this case, Brittany's inability to determine what is wrong. Her mind may be filled with possible causes, but without any facts (notice the woman in this card wearing a blindfold), she is forced into inaction. Her thoughts are causing her great distress, as shown in the Four of Swords.

The second row indicates that her husband is under a great deal of pressure. Here we find a battle card, the Six of Wands, as well as the Knight of Swords, a card that embodies aggressive and assertive action. The suit of wands can indicate spiritual or professional troubles, so it's possible there's a stressful situation unfolding in his workplace, or that he is dealing with something personal to him.

Because no cups appear in this layout, there is little chance that the distance Brittany is feeling from her husband is emotional, or has anything to do with their

The Reasons Reading
Brittany's Marriage

marriage. The real reason for the distance is represented by the Tower. This suggests trouble brewing at work or that Matt might be afraid of losing his job.

Emotionally, Brittany needs to avoid creating problems between herself and her husband. Because all the cards in the first row are swords, she may find herself stuck in a cycle of obsession. It will grow stronger if she continues to worry or ruminate over what might be going on. This could lead her to imagine all sorts of things. If her husband is in the midst of a struggle at work and she begins to constantly nag him or ask him what is wrong, it could worsen the situation, as evidenced by the Tower card in the final position of the layout.

Spiritually, Brittany must look within herself for resolution. The presence of the Page/Knave of Swords suggests an important message trying to emerge. Because she cannot access the answers intellectually (Two of Swords), she will need to seek spiritual retreat and guidance (Four of Swords) to calm her fears. She must find a way to trust her husband and support him through this difficult time by reopening the lines of communication between them. Once she realizes she is in no way responsible for his behavior, her fears will subside. While the Tower can predict an upset, the true message advises her to seek spiritual guidance in order to release, cleanse, and refresh her view of the situation.

Julia's Health Reading

Julia is trying to lose weight, but, each time she begins to make progress, she finds herself moving back up on the scales, resulting in more weight than when she started. She wants to discover the reason behind her inability to lose weight. Julia is a Gemini, so she selected the Queen of Swords as her significator card. The Queen of Swords represents air sign women.

She shuffled and then pulled the following cards:

> Significator—Queen of Swords
> Four of Pentacles
> Nine of Cups
> The Moon
> Ten of Cups
> The Lovers
> Eight of Cups

Notice that cups hold a dominant position in this reading, along with the Lovers and the Moon, all representative of emotions. This gives Julia an instant clue that the source of her troubles lies in her emotions, rather than any physiological or medical reasons.

The first card is the Four of Pentacles, which indicates holding onto or holding back from something or someone. In a health reading, it is also a card that can indicate someone carrying extra weight. Julia is aware of her need to lose weight, and is trying to do something about it. The amount of food or calories she is consuming (Nine of Cups) is far beyond what her body needs, but she has yet to admit this, and is operating under the illusion that her calorie intake is fine (the Moon).

In row two we look for clues about what is happening behind the scenes that could be influencing her inability to lose the weight. With the Ten of Cups and the Lovers in positions four and five, it's apparent Julia's relationship (or lack thereof) is the driving force in this equation. She may be caught in a troubled relationship, and is eating to avoid the reality that she needs to leave. Or, she may be unable to find a loving relationship, and believes it to be the source of her overeating. Another

The Reasons Reading
Julia's Health

possibility might be that her partner is sabotaging Julia's efforts by encouraging her to eat more or by bringing home food she has trouble resisting.

The final card, the Eight of Cups, confirms that before Julia can lose weight and keep it off, she will have to face her emotional issues (cups) and move beyond them. The Eight of Cups represents one's ability to leave current conditions and seek higher ground.

Emotionally, Julia may feel that she needs the weight as protection, portrayed by the Four of Pentacles. She may also feel deprived when she cannot have a certain food or enjoy herself from time to time (Nine of Pentacles). However, the Moon implies that Julia is overeating to avoid dealing with her emotional issues.

The Ten of Cups and the Lovers refer to issues Julia may have with experiencing love, for herself or another. If there have been failed relationships in the past, if her weight is keeping her from connecting with a loving partner, or if there was some type of abuse or neglect in childhood, these emotional aspects will play a part in Julia's reluctance to be free of the weight. Until she faces these issues and puts them behind her (Eight of Cups) with the help of a therapist, or through spiritual means, she will continue to struggle with this issue.

Spiritually, Julia is cutting herself off from her higher source of power when she overeats. Each time she diets and fails, she loses faith in herself and eats more, leaving her stuck in a metaphysical type of Catch-22. She could be afraid to let go of the extra food or the weight, based on the illusion that she needs it (Four of Pentacles, Nine of Cups and the Moon). Julia is keeping herself from the one thing she truly wants: a healthy and loving partnership. Before she can fulfill this dream, she must develop a partnership with Spirit. The image of the man who has turned his back on the past and dealt with his issues (Eight of Cups) illustrates that once she deals with these fears and emotional troubles from the past, she can turn to Spirit for help, ready to move into a brighter (and healthier) future.

BIRTHDAY/YEARLY FORECAST READING

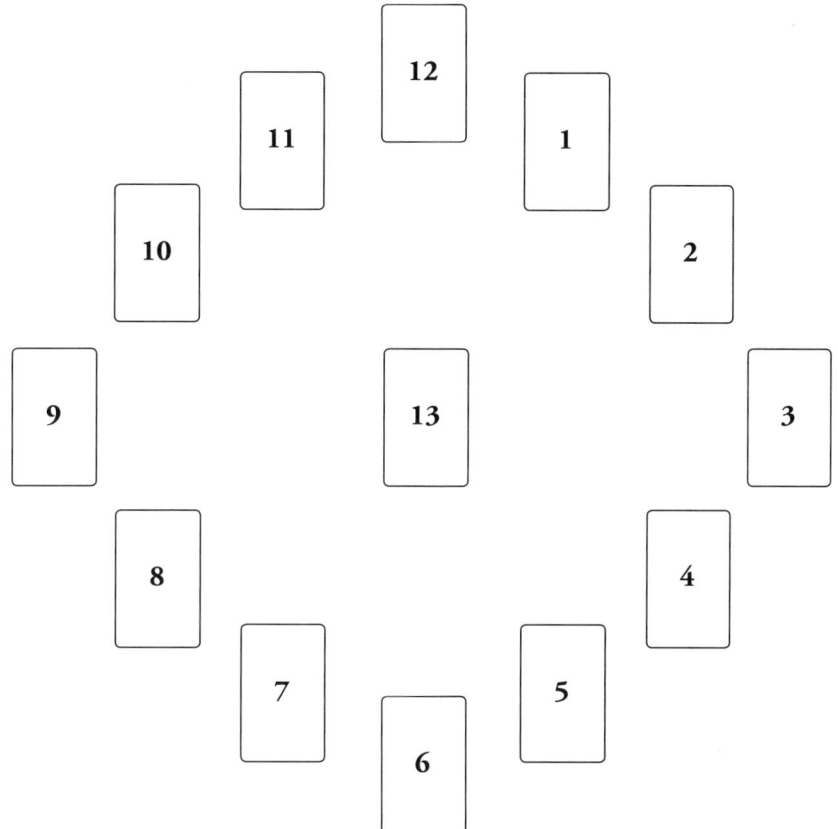

The Birthday/Yearly Forecast reading will challenge you to expand your knowledge of the various meanings of the cards, as a single card represents the energy of an entire month. This layout is typically used for birthday, anniversary, or New Year's readings, though you can perform one whenever you would like an overview of the twelve months ahead.

Keep in mind that this type of reading is of a more general tone, setting the stage for each month without going into detail. It can be helpful if you are trying to plan a major event during the next twelve months, for example, a wedding, vacation, or relocation. You can think of this reading as a metaphysical calendar, similar to wall calendars that feature a single picture for each month of the year.

Directions: As you shuffle the cards, concentrate on your hopes for the next twelve-month cycle. Fan them out across a table and pull thirteen cards at random or, draw them from the top of the deck. Shuffle the thirteen cards and then lay them out clockwise, placing the first card in the position that would represent one o'clock, as shown in the examples. Place the second card in the two o'clock position, and so on until you have laid out twelve cards. Place the thirteenth card in the middle. Card 1 will represent the current month, or January, when a new year begins.

Before you begin the reading, discuss with your querent their hopes and expectations for the twelve months ahead. In this way, you can watch for evidence of them while you read. Encourage your querent to be interactive with you during the reading, sharing any thoughts and feelings about what the cards might indicate.

For example, if your querent is hoping to move to a new home, watch for the Knight of Pentacles or the Four of Wands to appear. Querents and their partners who are trying to have a baby should watch for the Empress, the Moon, or the Queen of Pentacles to appear. For more guidance on which card combinations indicate specific events, refer to the card combinations table in appendix C.

Moving clockwise, interpret each card individually to determine the energy of that particular month. Notice any feelings or messages you get from the card. For example, if the first card is the Ace of Cups, the month will be emotionally full (cups represent emotion). New levels of self-love and unconditional love will evolve over the next thirty days. There is a possibility of new romance or the renewal of a current relationship. Study the image on the card more closely and discuss it with your querent for additional information.

Note that the months represented by major arcana cards will be more influential, and could indicate the coming of important events.

Feel free to pull one to three additional cards if you come across a card you have trouble deciphering, or if you desire more information about a particular month. Additional cards give you expanded insight and specifics about any month where the message seems vague or negative (cards such as the Devil, the Tower, Ten of Swords, Five of Wands, etc.).

When you have finished reading all twelve cards and their corresponding months, take a look at the card in the center. This card will contain the overall theme for the year ahead, and reveal the important lessons you or your querent will learn.

Sherilyn and Jack's Anniversary Reading

Sherilyn and Jack just celebrated their first wedding anniversary. Sherilyn would like to know what the next year holds for them.

After shuffling and fanning out the cards, she drew these thirteen cards:

Eight of Pentacles
Five of Cups—Five of Wands, Eight of Wands, the Tower
The Star
The High Priestess
King of Pentacles
Four of Swords
The Hermit
Knight of Swords
Page/Knave of Swords
The Magician
Four of Wands
Strength
The Lovers

Because Sherilyn and Jack's anniversary is in February, the card in the first position of this layout represents that month. The focus will be on their relationship, which dictates a certain tone for the reading. Remember, while you are contemplating the cards, always keep the theme of the question in mind.

The Eight of Pentacles resides in the February position. As the first card in this layout, it suggests that, over the last year, Sherilyn and Jack have become more adept at their relationship. They are focused on common goals and work to maintain a healthy relationship. Emotionally, their connection is thriving, as evidenced by the Eight of Pentacles (portrayed in this deck by a strong and blossoming plant). Spiritually, Jack and Sherilyn are committed to the relationship and work on building its foundation in loving ways, depicted on this card by the man working at the base of the plant.

Birthday/Yearly Forecast Reading
Sherilyn and Jack's Anniversary

The March position is occupied by the Five of Cups. It suggests a time of sorrow, though it is not specific as to the reason why. At this point, we drew three more cards to determine the source of this sorrow.

The cards that came up were the Five of Wands, the Eight of Wands and the Tower. Literally, this speaks to a possible fire in their home or the home of someone they love. This fire will start quickly (Eight of Wands) and, as the image suggests, could possibly be caused by arson or someone playing with matches. The Tower affirms an upsetting event of some kind. Based on the Tower and the image of the

BEGINNER READINGS | 63

gate that appears in the Eight of Wands, we can assume that the sadness predicted for March revolves around damage to a house. Because there are two wand cards present (wands carry the energy of fire), we see the possible cause as a fire. It will affect Sherilyn and Jack emotionally through the experience of loss. Spiritually, it will afford them a stronger appreciation for the blessings that they have, as tragedy often leads to a stronger connection with the Universe.

The Star inhabits the position of April. The Star is a wish card that promises a dream is about to come true. When I asked Sherilyn if she held a certain dream in her heart, she told me that the couple was hoping to have a child soon. With that information, I told her that April might be a month of increased fertility for her (based on the balanced jars of flowing water and sexual energy in the card), and that it was highly possible she could become pregnant during this month. Emotionally, this card represents inner joy, hope for the future, and contains the idea of "reaching for the stars" or "written in the stars." Spiritually, Sherilyn and Jack will be blessed in a karmic manner during this month, indicated by the image of a star hanging over the woman's head in this card.

May is represented by the High Priestess. Because a large Moon is depicted in the background of this image, we find more hints of the beginning of a pregnancy. The High Priestess is a card of wisdom and ancient knowledge. If Sherilyn discovers she is pregnant, she will begin collecting information from those who have had this experience. Emotionally, she will feel as if she has been blessed with a very important gift. This card also predicts that, in May, a new spiritual understanding will develop between the couple, and possibly a third spirit, not yet born.

The King of Pentacles rules over June. In this type of reading, the court cards represent traits or conditions normally associated with their suit rather than actual people. (See card combinations in appendix C for more detailed information.) The King of Pentacles represents mastery over physical and financial worlds. When we look at this card from an emotional standpoint, we interpret this marriage to be strong, stable, and secure. This is the month that Sherilyn and Jack could experience financial gain, and be able to start saving for the future. Spiritually, this card reminds them to take stock of their non-material riches. In this image, notice that the king lounges upon a pile of gold but his attention is on the future, where greater dreams await.

July is represented by the Four of Swords. This card indicates a time of rest and relaxation. If the couple is planning a vacation, this would be an ideal month to schedule it. Emotionally, both Sherilyn and Jack may feel drained and need to recharge. If Sherilyn is in fact pregnant, she will feel more tired than usual. Emotionally, there may be a lull in conversation or activity as, individually and together, they regroup. In a spiritual sense, the Four of Swords indicates a time of healing and inner transformation during which the couple can reconnect with the Divine.

August will be a time of enlightenment for this couple, designated by the Hermit card. Also known as the Seeker in some decks, this card implies a time of searching. In August, they will begin their search for a new house or perhaps new careers. Whatever desires have been building for the future, this is the time in which they can actively start to seek them out. Emotionally, they may feel isolated from each other or from their dreams, as their search could take longer than they expect. Spiritually, this is a fertile month for accessing new information and enlightenment, both of which will help the couple manifest their future goals.

The September position is occupied by the Knight of Swords. This could indicate a conflict or disagreement between Sherilyn and Jack, or could portray that assertive action will be necessary before they can move forward. Emotionally, they may find themselves short-tempered or stubborn. This card indicates the need to move quickly on something, perhaps to make an offer on a house or resolve an argument, rather than allowing it to build. Spiritually, they will have to release anger and resentment, striving for clearer communication and more unconditional love to reach a compromise in these conflicts.

The Page/Knave of Wands occupies the October position. This card heralds new inspiration or agreements in the partnership. Whatever issues arose in the previous month will have been resolved, so they can look forward to a fresh start. In this deck the Page stands facing a great expanse. The lizard on his cloak is symbolic of a dream this couple is ready to pursue. A new focus will emerge in Sherilyn and Jack's relationship, which could take the form of a new house, one or the other starting a new job, or collectively, a new goal to consider. Spiritually, this card represents spiritual growth and advancement, suggesting that new opportunities will come to them in karmic ways.

November is represented by the Magician. This major arcana card implies that November will be a powerful and transformational month for Sherilyn and Jack. Whatever they set their minds to, they can manifest, and karmic gifts are sure to come their way. If Sherilyn is not pregnant by this time, the possibility of conception is strong again this month. Emotionally, this couple will feel empowered, confident, and highly in tune with one another. Though the Magician card can sometimes imply deception, in this reading it speaks to the fact that spiritually, they have mastered all the elements of their relationship and can move together to create anything they desire.

With the Four of Wands in the December position, this could be the time when they purchase or move into a new house. As a card that represents home, family and security, Sherilyn and Jack will be focused on the holidays, personal relationships, and, hopefully, the imminent birth of their first child. Emotionally, they have much to be thankful for, and will mark the season by decorating their new home together for the first time. Spiritually, this card defines the protection of the Universe, and affirms that they have created a strong foundation from which to proceed.

The Strength card represents the energy of January, affirming continued growth and progress for Jack and Sherilyn. As they prepare to greet a new year, they will want to review the challenges they have overcome and the lessons they have learned together. The Strength card indicates power and determination, and, in this couple's case, increases their ability to maintain boundaries and stick with their disciplines. These traits will serve them well physically, emotionally, and spiritually in the coming months, as they become more secure and begin to expand their family and their assets. This card suggests their spiritual lives are strong, also contributing to their ability to manifest their dreams.

The Lovers card sits in the center of this reading, heralding a year of deepening love and affection. As partners, they will build great things together, spiritually as well as physically. Their emotional security comes from putting each other first while still maintaining their individuality. Spiritually, they will experience much joy this year. Notice the angel that hovers over the lovers in this card, suggesting a partnership not only between them, but in conjunction with Spirit, as they venture forward on a path to their dreams.

Dennis' Birthday Reading

Dennis is about to celebrate his fiftieth birthday, and would like to know what he can expect in the year ahead. The card in the number one position was designated as October, since this is the month in which he was born.

The thirteen cards he drew were:

The Hanged Man
Knight of Cups
The Empress
Knight of Pentacles
The Hierophant
Nine of Cups
Two of Wands
Four of Wands
Six of Cups
Seven of Swords
Ten of Cups
Six of Wands
Three of Cups

The Hanged Man occupies the first position and represents October. This card indicates a time of non-movement. Whatever projects or expectations Dennis has for this month will have to be put on hold. Though he may not like it, he will be blocked if he attempts to move forward. Emotionally, this card can indicate frustration, worry or indecision. Spiritually, this card is asking Dennis to go within this month, to experience a rebirth and transformation on a soul level.

In November we see the Knight of Cups. This indicates that action and movement will resume in November, particularly in personal matters and relationships. Because the knight is in the suit of cups, Dennis will be actively moving toward things that fulfill him emotionally. With a higher awareness (thanks to the inner work he completed in October), he will continue to advance spiritually as he integrates his intuition and emotions.

Birthday/Yearly Forecast Reading
Dennis' Birthday

The Empress card is in the December position. Dennis will spend most of his time celebrating the holidays with family and loved ones. Emotionally, the Empress will evoke his affectionate side and fill him with generosity. Spiritually, this card embodies the traits of a caregiver. This is the ideal season for Dennis to nurture himself and others, and act from the heart in all things.

Big changes await Dennis in January, as indicated by the Knight of Pentacles. Traditionally, the Knight of Pentacles refers to a physical move of some type. Dennis may decide to change his residence at this time, or move his business to a different location. This card can also indicate a restoration of health in January, so he may decide to join a gym or take up a sport to improve his energy and mobility. Emotionally, the Knight of Pentacles represents one who is ready for change, inside and out. Spiritually, this card speaks to Dennis' intuitive ability to clear the blocks in his way this month so he can move confidently into the future.

The Hierophant occupies the February position. This card represents the wisdom of following directions and aligning to a higher authority. Dennis has his own business, but may have to address issues of licensing, permits, or other regulatory obligations related to his work. He would be wise to stay away from any get-rich-quick schemes, and follow the tried-and-true methods that have brought him success in the past. Spiritually, the Hierophant calls for a return to his spiritual disciplines, and asks that Dennis devote more time to expanding his intuitive awareness.

The Nine of Cups is in the March position. This will be an abundant month for Dennis, with much to celebrate. It indicates that more than one success or blessing will appear. Emotionally, a sense of joy will surround his every move. Dennis is single, but desires a relationship. With the Nine of Cups in this position, it could be a fortunate month for him in the love department. This card represents spiritual abundance and a renewed sense that he is being aided by the Universe to move closer to his dreams. He may find that, almost overnight, a single effort will begin to generate multiple gifts, courtesy of Spirit.

Dennis will have an important decision to make in April, as indicated by the Two of Wands. This card indicates a job offer or business proposal, which would involve leaving one position to pursue another. Emotionally, this will be a time of transition as Dennis releases one choice and embraces another. He may find himself at a crossroads of sorts. Because both choices may be equally appealing, he will have to rely on intuition and spiritual guidance for direction on how best to proceed.

The Four of Wands represents May. This could prove a lucrative month for Dennis, as he is in the business of selling houses (a house is one definition of this card). The Four of Wands indicates a strong foundation and the building of one's security. It can also refer to his desire to start a family. Emotionally, the Four of Wands indicates that he will feel less scattered and more structured in his approach to life during this month. Spiritually, the Four of Wands confirms that Dennis is surrounded by spiritual forces that encourage his success and protect his movements.

June is represented by the Six of Cups. This card speaks to the idea of a soul mate or new friend. If Dennis didn't meet someone in March, this is another month where a love connection is possible. If he is already involved with someone, this could be the month the relationship becomes more serious. Emotionally, this month will herald more play and less work. If Dennis was planning a vacation this year, I'd recommend June as a positive option, based on this card. Spiritually, the Six of Cups supports the idea of simply being in the world, and encourages Dennis to live each day with childlike joy and optimism.

Dennis will have to practice extra caution in July, based on the Seven of Swords in this position. This card indicates stealing or thievery, and if Dennis is not careful, he could lose something of value to him. Emotionally, someone close to him could betray or undermine him. This could be a family, romantic, or business connection. Spiritually, he needs to ask Spirit for extra protection and higher awareness. Then, if someone tries to steal from him on a physical, emotional, or spiritual level, he will be alerted by his intuition.

The August position is occupied by the Ten of Cups. This card speaks to a month of love and abundance. Because the Six of Cups appeared in June, this card confirms that a developing relationship will prosper and grow. Dennis could be thinking about marriage or a more permanent connection during this month. This card embodies the concepts of affection, true love, and joy, predicting that his relationships will endure and that he will experience contentment. Spiritually, he will feel at one with the Universe this month, protected and supported.

September is represented by the Six of Wands. This card suggests that Dennis will be facing some battles. On a positive note, forewarned is forearmed, so alerting him to this fact can help him prepare for whatever may happen. This card also indicates an improvement in his health and a stronger constitution. Emotionally, Dennis may have to defend his dreams. The Six of Wands promises that he will remain clear, focused, and determined. Spiritually, Dennis has the support of the Universe behind him, and is ready to meet the challenges that come his way. With Spirit's help, he will breeze through these battles, and is sure to emerge victorious.

The card in the center of the layout is the Three of Cups. As the central theme of this reading, the Three of Cups predicts more socializing and advancement this year. It also addresses Dennis' need to expand his contacts, socially as well as professionally. Emotionally, he will experience three major breakthroughs in matters of the heart. Spiritually, Dennis will complete this year feeling freer, more joyful, and one step closer to his quest for inner as well as outer wholeness. Dennis will feel divinely blessed, calling for celebration, the traditional meaning of this card.

Jon's New Year Reading

Jon has had many challenges in his personal life over the last two years, and, as a new year approaches, is hoping to see improvement in the areas of health, finance, and relationships.

For this New Year's reading, he drew the following thirteen cards:

>   Ace of Swords
>   The Lovers
>   Ten of Wands
>   Five of Cups
>   Knight of Pentacles
>   Death
>   The Moon
>   Two of Cups
>   The Hanged Man
>   Eight of Pentacles
>   The High Priestess
>   Eight of Cups
>   The Empress

At first glance, this appears to be another difficult year for Jon. Six months in this reading contain major arcana cards, and six of the cards in the overall layout indicate challenging times. As such, this is when using the multiple metaphysical meanings will come in handy. As Jon faces a year of transformation, Spirit will ask him to let go of whatever situations are keeping him stuck, so he can restore balance and prosperity to his life.

Because this reading is specific to a new calendar year, the first card will represent January. The Ace of Swords reveals a stronger and more determined Jon, ready to do whatever it takes to change his life. The ace speaks to new beginnings, while the suit of swords, to new thoughts and ideas. Emotionally, he feels optimistic about the future and the new year ahead. During this month he will gain new awareness from the Universe that will help him recognize and prepare to move beyond anything that is not positive in his life.

Birthday/Yearly Forecast Reading
Jon's New Year

The Lovers occupies February. Jon has been involved in a relationship for five years, which has had many ups and downs. He has been thinking about ending it. However, during this month, the connection will be emotionally fulfilling and stable, and both parties will be ready to give the partnership a second chance. Spiritually, this card will encourage Jon to view his partner and himself with more unconditional love, affection, and appreciation.

In March, Jon could be overburdened with work obligations, as depicted by the Ten of Wands. He may experience a few weeks of overtime, or be faced with taking on others' responsibilities. This could work against him in his relationship, for he will have little time for himself or anyone else. Emotionally, he could become short-tempered or impatient. Spiritually, there is a transition in the works, as the Universe attempts to strengthen his resolve and skills, while shifting his focus away from other areas of his life.

April is represented by the Five of Cups. Because cups rule emotions, and the five card represents a loss of some kind, there is a strong possibility that his relationship will end. This is also confirmed by the fact that his relationship does not show up again in the remaining cards for the year, and amplified by his confession that there has been trouble in the past. Emotionally, a brighter future lies ahead (depicted in this card by the two upright cups on the right), once he has released what is no longer viable. The Five of Cups speaks to a time of spiritual release, which will be vital to Jon's ability to move forward.

In the May position, we find the Knight of Pentacles. This card represents a physical move on someone's part. Either Jon or his partner will be moving out. More than likely Jon will be moving, as this reading is specific to him, but, either way, his surroundings will be in transition. Emotionally, he will experience a shift, and, by the end of the month, Jon will be able to appreciate the changes that take place in his environment. Spiritually, one of Jon's requests to the Universe was to improve his relationship, and though it seems to contradict his desires, he must let go of what he has to access what he wants—a loving and devoted connection.

The Death card occupies the June position. This month will herald a rebirth for Jon, as one aspect of his life (the relationship) fades away to make room for new opportunities. Emotionally, he may feel lost or surrounded by sadness, but in the midst of this transition, Jon will reconnect with aspects of himself that may have been lost or buried while he and his partner were together. Slowly but surely, his true self will return as Spirit leads him through a tunnel of darkness and into a brand new awareness of life and its endless potentials.

July is represented by the Moon, a card that traditionally predicts illusion or self-deception. Jon must be mindful not to fall into addictive behavior or activities that distract him from his spiritual cycle of growth. He may want to seek help to deal with his emotions or the fear that he will never find another relationship, common when one finds themselves in this position. He may also hear from his past lover during this month, and must be careful not to let his emotions lead him back into a no-win situation. Spiritually, the Moon card calls for Jon to trust his intuition over his emotions or ego, and warns him to avoid getting caught up in the outer trappings of life.

The Two of Cups promises a return to emotional balance for Jon in August. At this point, he may begin to date again or receive romantic attention from someone new. Though the connection may not be long-term, it will restore Jon's confidence. His experience with this new person will help Jon become clearer on the type of partnership he wants. Spiritually, this card represents a promise of hope and optimism for the future, a sign that he is ready to put the past behind him and open up to new experiences as the Universe presents them.

The Hanged Man represents September. This card indicates that most aspects of Jon's life will hang in limbo. Because he will have time on his hands this month, he can regroup, recover, and start making plans for the future. September could also be a good month to get away for a vacation or involve himself in spiritual practices that will continue to improve his perspective of the future. Because he mentioned health issues at the start of this reading, this would be an ideal time to address any conditions that might involve surgery or recovery time. The Hanged Man also calls for spiritual reflection, patience and self-examination, all activities he should engage in during this recovery process.

The Eight of Pentacles sits in the October position. This card predicts a promotion or career advancement for Jon. Based on all the hard work he did in March and the skills he has learned since then, Jon has become very adept at his work. He may even start an independent business. Whatever path he chooses, more money appears to be coming his way. This will restore his financial balance, one of the areas he mentioned struggling with in previous years. Once money is no longer an issue, his emotions will return to balance as well. Spiritually, he is finally being recognized and rewarded by his employers, along with the Universe, for his willingness to let go of what no longer works for him, and for his ability to embrace and practice new spiritual disciplines.

The High Priestess appears in the November position. This suggests a time of enlightenment in which Jon will gain new awareness and appreciation for the gifts that are beginning to emerge from his past struggles. His emotions will no longer be a source of discomfort, but will offer him important messages instead. Spiritually, Jon's intuition will grow stronger, enabling him to make better choices about his life and his future as he continues to follow Spirit's directives.

In December, the Eight of Cups suggests Jon has finally overcome his challenges and is ready to move to higher ground. He will come to the end of this difficult cycle and be ready to leave the past behind. Jon's future looks bright, with endless options ahead. Now that his emotional and financial challenges have been resolved, he may also discover that most of his health problems have corrected themselves. (The cups in this image imply that whatever difficulties he had at the beginning of the year have been resolved and are behind him.) Spiritually, the majority of his troubles stemmed from his inability to let go of ideas and situations that were bad for him. Now that he's surrounded by spiritual protection and abundance, his choices will begin to work in his favor, delivering the outcomes he's hoping for.

The final card, located in the center of the layout, is the Empress. This sets the theme of Jon's year as one of self-nurturing and personal care. The Empress embodies an energy of comfort and support that will enable him to move through the year's emotional situations with grace. Spiritually, the Empress will teach him to honor his truths, love himself, and trust that he has a benevolent parent in the Universe. As his difficulties clear and he finds himself on the brink of a new life, he can create a brighter future, free of strife and burdens.

Two
INTERMEDIATE READINGS

INVERTED PYRAMID READING

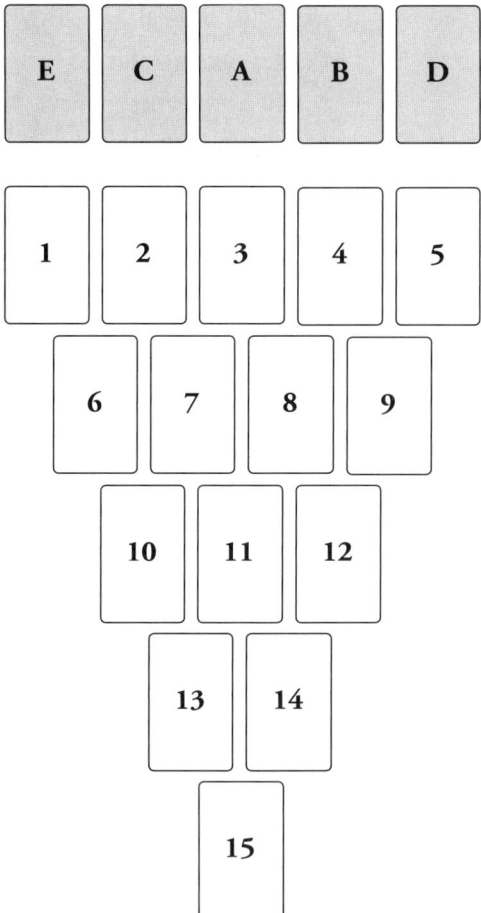

The Inverted Pyramid reading is ideal for general readings or for querents who have a series of questions they would like to address. There is no need to reshuffle the cards for each subject or question. After you complete one layout, you can move the cards aside and begin to address the next topic with the remaining cards in the piles. This reading is highly effective for practitioners who do a majority of their work over the phone or internet, and do not have time to reshuffle the cards for each question.

Directions: Ask the querent to concentrate on his or her questions as the cards are shuffled. The deck will then be divided into five piles (as shown in the illustrations), beginning with the middle pile (A) and alternating on either side to create the five cuts (B, C, D, and E). The piles are laid face down and will be of varying depths, as the cards will break naturally at specific points. (Note: If at some point in the reading you run out of cards in one pile, you can pull a group of cards off the top of another pile to replenish it. Use your intuition to determine which pile to draw from and how many cards to move.)

Draw one card from each pile, face up, to form the first row of five cards. These cards define and acknowledge the present circumstances or recent past. This row will also verify that the cards are addressing the question that has been asked.

To create the second row, draw one card each from piles E, C, B, and D, skipping over pile A. Lay them under the first five cards, as shown in the illustrations to begin forming the inverted pyramid. The cards in this row will reveal what is most likely to happen next, or offer direction on the best way to proceed.

The third row is created by drawing one card each from piles E, A, and D. Lay them beneath the second row so they touch the upper cards and continue the pyramid effect. These cards represent hidden factors of which the querent is unaware. These cards may present issues that the querent has the power to change, or reveal things that are governed by destiny and cannot be changed.

The fourth and fifth rows are drawn together and read as a whole. To create the fourth row, draw cards from the C and B piles, placing them below row three as shown. The fifth row consists of a single card from the A pile, completing the inverted pyramid. These three cards are read as a group and contain the probable outcome, advice, and additional information to answer the querent's question.

As you read the cards, try to formulate a connection between the series of cards in each row. For every card you interpret, the one following it will add to the unfolding story. You can go back and forth between the cards, looking for connections that will enable you to interpret each row and form a complete concept or idea to present to the querent.

Mini Inverted Pyramid Reading

For a quicker reading, divide the deck into three piles rather than five. Select the top three cards to form the first row (the situation), one card each from the left and right piles to create the second row (hidden aspects), and one card from the center pile to form the third row (the outcome or advice).

Pauline's Writing Career Reading

Pauline has been working on a number of writing projects, hoping to have one of them published. She would like to know where to focus, which projects have the most potential, and if one of her projects will be picked up by a publisher. After shuffling the cards, she divided them into five piles.

These were the five cards drawn for the first row of the layout:

The Hermit
The Lovers
The Empress
Seven of Swords
Seven of Wands

The first thing we notice is that three of the cards in this row are major arcana, and the other two are sevens. (Remember that major arcana cards carry a stronger message.) Because the first row addresses the current situation, the cards here suggest that there is something Pauline needs to be aware of (the Hermit). In this card, the man is shining a light into the darkness, looking for something. The next card is the Lovers. Because this is a business question, the Lovers represent either a business partner or someone to whom she has submitted one or more of her manuscripts. The next card, the Empress, implies that the person she needs to look at more closely is a woman. Since Pauline is working on a project with someone who is female, (as well as a mother, indicated by the Empress), this woman may be the most likely to consider. Next to her is the Seven of Swords, which can represent some form of stealing. Since this question falls in the realm of publishing, it appears that there may be a copyright infringement, or the person may be "stealing" some of Pauline's ideas. The Seven of Wands lands in the next position, suggesting that Pauline needs to protect herself and her work.

Emotionally, these cards suggest that Pauline may be too trusting, and could be taken advantage of. To prevent her ideas from being stolen, these cards have taken an unexpected direction to send her an immediate warning. When this happens, address it right away, discussing the possibilities of deceit with your querent. As you

Inverted Pyramid Reading
Pauline's Writing Career

continue the reading, the rest of the cards should answer the specific question your querent has asked.

Reviewing these cards from a spiritual angle, the Hermit reminds Pauline to rely on her intuition to determine which of her current projects holds the most promise. The Lovers signify that writing is Pauline's true passion, and that the Universe supports her dreams, as indicated by the Angel at the top of the card. In a spiritual sense, the combination of the Empress and the Seven of Swords implies that her obligations as a mother are preventing Pauline from writing as often as she would like. She needs to ask Spirit to help her defend her position (Seven of Wands), set boundaries around her time, and continue working toward her goal of becoming a published author.

In row two, the following cards were drawn:

Queen of Cups
Ace of Swords
King of Wands
Eight of Wands

This series of cards reveals what should happen next regarding Pauline's work. The Queen of Cups represents Pauline, a Scorpio. The queen is gazing into a cup she holds in her hands, suggesting that the project she is currently working on or has just completed has the greatest potential to be published. The Ace of Swords indicates a message or offer arriving from a business man (King of Wands) within two weeks (Eight of Wands). When the Eight of Wands appears in a general reading, it is normally interpreted as a card that predicts something coming in quickly, typically in short timeframes in "twos"—two hours, two days, or two weeks, as a rule.

Emotionally, Pauline must continue to move forward with heartfelt hope (Queen of Cups). The Ace of Swords reflects her optimistic belief that, when the time is right, doors will open and victory will be hers. The King and Eight of Wands represent her undying passion and determination to have her work published.

Spiritually, the Queen of Cups asks Pauline to continue in her quest and trust in the Universe's timing, as it predicts that soon her writings will reach the person who can bring them to life (represented by the Ace of Swords). Once she connects with this individual (King of Wands), the Universe will begin to move her dreams ahead quickly (Eight of Wands).

Row three reveals aspects of Pauline's process she may be unaware of. This information can alert her to any changes needed, and encourage her if it reveals how close she is to manifesting her dream.

The cards drawn were:

Eight of Cups
High Priestess
Nine of Wands

These cards predict that Pauline is already moving to a higher level (Eight of Cups). It is possible that unbeknownst to her, someone is already interested in her work. This person is embodied in the High Priestess card, and may represent either a publisher or a literary agent to whom she has been submitting samples of her work. With this person behind her, Pauline will have her work read by the right people (Nine of Wands).

Emotionally, these cards encourage Pauline to continue improving her manuscripts and her writing, even if success is still elusive (Eight of Cups). With each new project, she becomes more skilled and perceptive (the High Priestess). As she continues to create, her inspiration for future projects will grow and evolve (Nine of Wands).

Spiritually, the Eight of Cups indicates Pauline's commitment to her passion for writing, while leaving the end results up to the Universe. Pauline continued to pursue her dreams when nothing happened with her first manuscript, and this card reflects her enduring spiritual drive to move toward higher ground. Pauline's work carries important wisdom and will be of value in the world (suggested by the High Priestess). She is strengthening her spiritual awareness and power with each new manuscript she writes (indicated by the Nine of Wands).

The fourth and fifth rows consisted of:

>Page/Knave of Pentacles
>Three of Wands
>Seven of Cups

As advice and answer cards, it is best to read these as a group. The Page/Knave of Pentacles represents a message coming to Pauline that could involve a book deal or an offer of money. The Three of Wands reminds her that all she needs to do now is stand back and wait for this message to arrive. Because the Seven of Cups sits in the final position, she could be overwhelmed by the offer or, quite possibly, receive other offers from different sources all at once. The Seven of Cups can represent worry or one who has too many things on their mind. In Pauline's case, the acceptance of her manuscript could overwhelm her, but in a positive way.

Emotionally, she should be able to maintain her balance (Page/Knave of Pentacles), her patience (Three of Wands), and her family obligations (Seven of Cups), no matter what occurs during this process.

Spiritually, Pauline must keep her focus on the present, and what is in front of her (Page/Knave of Pentacles), spend more time in meditation or contemplation (Three of Wands), and allow the Universe to expand her life when the time is right. The Seven of Cups also indicates that multiple opportunities could karmically appear all at once.

Reviewing the overall messages in this reading, we can see that Pauline is definitely on the road to being published, and simply needs to continue what she is doing—creating with passion, and trusting the Universe to make her dreams come true. She needs to watch out for deception and protect her ideas. The cards also suggest that setting new boundaries with her family will be essential, so she can create more time for her writing. Her efforts are supported and encouraged by Spirit, so she must continue to follow her calling.

Charlotte's Relationship Reading

Charlotte has been dating Paul for six years. They have been living together for three years, and Charlotte wants to get married. Paul is reluctant to do so and keeps putting the matter off. Though they are very happy, she will not feel secure until they are married. She wants to know if she should continue to wait for Paul to marry her, give him an ultimatum, or walk away.

The following cards were drawn for row one:

> Three of Cups
> Judgement
> The Devil
> Temperance
> Ten of Cups

Row one represents the current situation. Note that the row begins and ends with cups (emotions) and that the three middle cards are all major arcana. This speaks to a loving relationship, but affirms that there are important issues between them creating an imbalance. The Three of Cups indicates that Charlotte and Paul are very happy together, but that Charlotte is expecting a proposal (Judgement) that has yet to come. The Devil reveals that this is creating fear and concern, and could be making Charlotte question Paul's feelings and his level of commitment. The Temperance card requests that she be patient, and the Ten of Cups reminds her that, except for this issue, their relationship is a happy one.

Emotionally, note that the Devil sits in the center position, but is surrounded by positive cards. This commitment issue appears to be the only troublesome aspect of their relationship. Charlotte's fear and frustration could be the very thing that is making Paul hold back. It is possible that if Charlotte can change her approach and her feelings about marriage, she will also affect Paul's feelings about making a permanent commitment.

Metaphysically, the fastest way to change what someone else is doing is to change what we are doing. Spiritually, this row is pointing out that Charlotte's focus has become controlling, with fear (the Devil) causing her to manipulate the situation to

Inverted Pyramid Reading
Charlotte's Relationship

create a particular outcome, within a certain time. Although six years is a long time to wait for a permanent commitment, Charlotte will have to go within herself and address this issue spiritually in order to resolve it.

The following cards were pulled for row two, indicating what will happen next:

Knight of Pentacles
The Empress
Six of Wands
The Fool

The Knight of Pentacles foretells that a change is coming. A movement to a more secure and committed relationship is in process, confirmed by the Empress, who in this deck, holds a large golden ring with a cross on the bottom (the astrological symbol for Venus). Looking at the image, one thinks of a ring, so Charlotte can take this as a positive sign that her dream is within reach. The Six of Wands can represent the six years they have been together. (It is a good practice to note the numbers on the cards as references for timing, especially if one number repeats itself.) This card is also considered a battle card that promises a positive outcome. Because the Fool occupies the next position in the row, the combination of these two cards implies a victory as soon as Charlotte redirects her efforts to create a new cycle in the relationship.

From an emotional standpoint, these cards tell Charlotte that if she changes her approach (Knight of Pentacles) by standing still and letting her feminine powers do all the work (the Empress), Paul will be inspired (Six of Wands) to move their relationship to the next level (the Fool).

Spiritually, the cards also call for change. Notice that the Knight of Pentacles holds his shield up as if to block himself, while the Empress holds a very different type of shield in front of her, one that is open and carries an inviting quality. This indicates that if Charlotte drops her defenses and opens herself up to the relationship spiritually, she can inspire Paul to move forward without any further effort on her part. If Charlotte can release her fears and turn the situation over to Spirit, the blocked energy between the two of them will disappear almost immediately.

Row three reveals hidden aspects or influences Charlotte is unaware of. Here we have:

Five of Swords
Justice
Queen of Pentacles

The Five of Swords indicates that either Charlotte or Paul (or both) have had failed relationships in the past. Because Paul appears resistant to marriage and the Justice card appears next to the Five of Swords, I would ask Charlotte at this point if Paul has been married before, and if the marriage ended in divorce. The Justice card often represents a legal situation and the Five of Swords usually appears in a relationship reading when a separation or divorce has occurred. (See card combinations in appendix C).

Following these cards is the Queen of Pentacles, who represents a particular person. Charlotte is an Aquarius, and would, if this card referred to her, appear as the Queen of Swords. (See significator cards in appendix B for more information.) Although she may not know Paul's ex-wife's birth date, we can assume that this queen represents the ex-wife. We can also assume that because pentacles represent money, his ex-wife may have received much of their financial holdings in the divorce. With this information, we can see that Paul's reluctance to marry Charlotte may have more to do with fear of financial loss, rather than any emotional reason.

However, Paul could not yet have recovered emotionally from his divorce and may in fact still be trying to regain his financial balance. He will not feel safe and secure enough to move forward until he resolves this. It is important to note that because his reluctance has nothing to do with Charlotte, it could be the reason her requests to make this relationship permanent have fallen on deaf ears.

Spiritually, the Five of Swords in this row is asking Charlotte to consider Paul's side and to remember that what he has gone through is the very thing that brought him to her. Had he not divorced, they would never have met, much less formed their current union. When she stands back to consider things from a more balanced perspective (Justice), she will realize that she already possesses Paul's heart and devotion (Queen of Pentacles), no matter what kind of legal commitment has been made.

Rows four and five contain the following cards:

Two of Pentacles
Queen of Swords
The Chariot

Note that seven of the fifteen cards (almost half) that we pulled for this reading are major arcana. This tells us that the cards are sending a powerful and life-changing message to help Charlotte resolve this issue.

The Two of Pentacles suggests that Paul has already considered asking Charlotte to marry him. With the Queen of Swords (Charlotte) showing up next to the Two of Pentacles, Paul knows how important this is to her, and is attempting to look at things from a more balanced perspective. He does nothing in haste, but is considering all angles of how to proceed. The Chariot sits in the final position, indicating that there will be positive movement in this situation.

If Charlotte will work on stabilizing her emotions by releasing fear and agreeing to wait just a bit longer, things will soon begin to move forward. She does not have to do anything except turn the focus back to herself, and allow the relationship to reach its commitment stage naturally.

Spiritually, trusting in the spiritual connection Charlotte and Paul already have is the key to resolving this issue. Note that the Two of Pentacles as well as the Chariot ask this couple to consider both sides of the impasse along with each other's feelings. In this situation, Charlotte's willingness to let go of the drive to be married and turn it over to Spirit will move this relationship toward a stronger and more committed partnership.

Clarence's Health Reading

Clarence has been experiencing health problems over the past six months but can't seem to locate the source of his troubles. He has seen a number of doctors who say the same thing—everything looks fine. He complains about a lack of energy, headaches, sharp pains in his lower back, and insomnia. He would like to find out whether these health issues are physical, emotional, or spiritual, and what he can do to alleviate them.

The cards he pulled for the first row of the layout were:

The Hermit
Four of Wands
Two of Swords
Knight of Swords
Two of Wands

These cards affirm Clarence's frustration at not being able to discover the source of his health problems. The Hermit portrays his search for answers, while the Four of Wands represents the four symptoms he is complaining about. Note that, coming directly after the Hermit card, the Four of Wands speaks of the return to health he is seeking. Followed by the Two of Swords, which addresses his inability to discover the causes behind these four symptoms. Again, pay close attention when you see a card which reflects a number that has already been established in the question or reading. (If he suffered from three symptoms, a number three card should appear, etc.) The Knight of Swords reveals the frustration and anger Clarence feels about his inability to resolve these issues. The Two of Wands suggests that he is at a crossroads, ready to look beyond modern medicine to discover whether these problems are truly physical or could have a metaphysical, emotional, or spiritual source.

Emotionally, Clarence continues to operate in the dark (the Hermit) despite his best efforts. The Four of Wands suggests he's learning to live with these problems, even though they could be causing depression (Two of Swords) and resentment (Knight of Swords). Clarence is at the end of his rope and ready to find some kind of resolution (Two of Wands).

Inverted Pyramid Reading
Clarence's Health

Spiritually, the Hermit suggests that Clarence look inward to resolve these issues. While the problems are definitely affecting his foundation of well-being (Four of Wands), his outside search for answers continues to leave him in the dark (Two of Swords.) He is willing to take a different action to resolve them (Knight of Swords) and is now seeking spiritual direction (Two of Wands) through this reading.

The next four cards will advise Clarence as to what he should do next:

King of Pentacles
Seven of Swords
Strength
Wheel of Fortune

INTERMEDIATE READINGS | 95

Looking at these cards from a health perspective, the King of Pentacles suggests that one of these symptoms is, indeed, physical. (Pentacles rule physical and material aspects of life.) Swords can often indicate back troubles, so with the Seven of Swords in the next position, this row suggests that Clarence investigate this particular area of his body. The Strength card indicates that there may be some weakness in his back, and that a visit to a professional who specializes in this area (a chiropractor or orthopedist) could help. In turn, it may improve or eliminate the other symptoms Clarence is experiencing (Wheel of Fortune), and provide instant relief.

Though Clarence has been emotionally frustrated by past visits to doctors, the Strength and Wheel of Fortune cards suggest that once again he seek professional help for his back problem (Seven of Swords). By narrowing his focus to this one area of pain, the cards imply that a specialist (King of Pentacles) should be able to resolve his most pressing health problem.

Spiritually, we can read the Strength and Wheel of Fortune cards as signs that resolution is coming Clarence's way, and that he should continue his quest to resolve these problems. The Seven of Swords cautions Clarence not to engage in negative thinking, false medical diagnostics, or begin to feel that his situation is hopeless. The King of Pentacles and the Strength cards promise that spiritual intervention is at hand.

The third row reveals hidden aspects that may be contributing to the situation. Here we find:

The Magician
King of Swords
Six of Pentacles

These three cards suggest that Clarence has been trusting in the wrong people; in this case, indifferent doctors (the Magician). The King of Swords represents Clarence, a Libra, while the Six of Pentacles affirms that in his search for answers, he has been investing a lot of money in the wrong people. (Note that because these cards show up in the row of hidden influence or things he may not realize, we look for aspects of his situation that portray a misunderstanding on his part. Had these cards come up in the previous or following rows, they would have had a completely different meaning. For example, if they were located in rows four or five, the Magician might indicate that Clarence will find a doctor who can work "magic" on the situation.)

Emotionally, he has been looking to the wrong people (Magician) and depending on them for answers (Six of Pentacles), only to find himself back where he started (King of Swords). This is the hidden reason that things have not been resolved.

Spiritually, this row is asking Clarence to review his futile attempts of the past, and to learn from the fact that they haven't worked. Continuing to seek help from the same people will only create more frustration. It speaks to the adage, "If nothing changes, nothing changes." The Magician and King of Swords combine to request that he think differently, while the Six of Pentacles implies there are other options out there, yet to be explored.

Notice that at this point, no emotional or spiritual causes have come to light as the source of Clarence's physical complaints.

The final two rows (4 and 5) contain these cards:

Ace of Swords
Knight of Wands
The Star

The Ace of Swords reaffirms that, if Clarence will address his back issue with the right kind of doctor, he will find relief. His pain will lessen and his energy will be restored (Knight of Wands). His wish to return to balanced health is assured by the appearance of the Star.

Emotionally, he will have to make one more effort to resolve this, indicated by both the Ace of Swords and the Knight of Wands. Once he does, the Star card predicts a full recovery.

Spiritually, these three cards assure Clarence that there is a simple way to resolve all of his issues by addressing the single most debilitating one (Ace of Swords), and that the actions he takes will be supported by the Universe (Knight of Wands). The Star verifies that a breakthrough is on the way, and that Clarence now has the spiritual awareness and direction he needs to rid himself of this debilitating cycle of health problems.

THE RELATIONSHIP READING

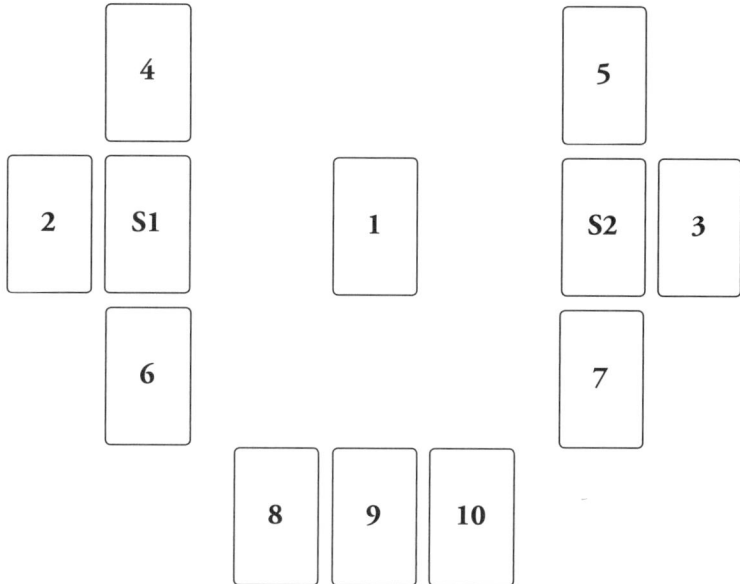

The Relationship Reading focuses on love relationships, but can also be used to investigate all types of partnerships, as it reveals the true purpose, motives and intentions of these connections. Whether you are delving into a relationship between a man and a woman, two men, two women, a business partnership, parent and child, or between friends, this reading can bring greater understanding to both parties as it reveals karmic reasons for coming together.

Directions: Select a significator (see significator tables in appendix B) to represent the two people in the relationship. If you are reading for a male/female relationship, place the female significator in the left-hand position and the male on the right. If the reading involves a same-sex relationship, you can place the significator card in either position. If you find yourself reading for two people of the same sex who are represented by the same element of the zodiac in the significator tables (i.e., a Cancer man and a Scorpio man, both represented by the King of Cups), you can select either the queen or knight of that suit to signify one of them.

Once you have selected the significators, place them side by side, leaving space in between for a center card, as shown in the illustration.

Shuffle the remaining cards as you concentrate on the relationship. Draw the cards and lay them out in the order shown.

- Card 1 identifies the karmic connection, theme, or higher purpose of this relationship
- Card 2 indicates what is moving significator 1 toward significator 2
- Card 3 indicates what is moving significator 2 toward significator 1
- Card 4 reveals how significator 1 regards the relationship
- Card 5 reveals how significator 2 regards the relationship
- Card 6 outlines the foundation or basis for significator 1's feelings about the relationship
- Card 7 outlines the foundation or basis for significator 2's feelings about the relationship
- Cards 8, 9, and 10 will reveal the next stage of development and general outlook for the relationship

Emma and Mark's Love Reading

Emma and Mark met on a blind date and agree it was love at first sight—they've been inseparable ever since. Because things happened so quickly, Mark is curious to know if there are past-life connections between them, and if their relationship has a solid foundation. Mark is a Cancer and Emma is a Capricorn, so he selected the King of Cups as his significator and the Queen of Pentacles as her significator.

The cards he drew for this reading were:

Significator 1—Queen of Pentacles
Significator 2—King of Cups
The Star
Knight of Wands
Three of Pentacles
King of Pentacles
The Lovers
Knight of Swords
Ten of Cups
The Empress
Ace of Swords
Two of Wands

The Star appears in the number 1 position between Emma and Mark. This affirms that the relationship is a wish come true for both of them. Emotionally, their union holds much joy and a promising future. Because they met under karmic circumstances, the Star also suggests that Spirit was behind the timing and manner in which they came together.

Behind Emma in the number 2 position, we have the Knight of Wands. As the card that moves her toward Mark, it verifies she is filled with emotional passion and desire. Spiritually, it speaks to the soulful connection she feels with Mark.

The Three of Pentacles sits behind Mark in the number 3 position, and reveals he is ready to invest in a relationship in which he can grow and prosper. Emotionally, he is on new ground and has never before experienced such strong feelings, as

Relationship Reading
Emma and Mark's Love

implied by the "internship" nature of this card. Spiritually, the Three of Pentacles represents new experience and the opportunity to grow, thanks to the influence of another person.

Looking at the cards in this row as a whole, we see three of the four elements of life represented. The fire (Knight of Wands), earth (Queen and Three of Pentacles) and water (King of Cups) elements that appear here speak to a well-rounded emotional connection, supported by the major arcana card the Star, located in the center. Spiritually, this grouping represents a positive balance of physical, emotional, and karmic energy, all essential to an enduring union. With the Star card in the middle, acting as the karmic "glue" or higher purpose of this relationship, there is spiritual support for Mark and Emma to be together.

Next we consider what each person thinks about the other. The King of Pentacles is in position 4, above Emma's head. She considers Mark to be strong, confident, grounded, and stable. We can see she has positive feelings for the man she's in love with. Above Mark's head in position 5, we have the Lovers, an indicator of his devotion and affection for Emma.

Emotionally, they are on the same wavelength, grateful to have each other in their lives. Based on these cards, both feel an added sense of security, support, and fulfillment in this relationship.

Spiritually, we look to the Lovers as a definite sign that the Universe supports this love relationship, and intends for it to be long-term. Neither Mark nor Emma carries a hidden agenda, though they may both view this relationship idealistically, based on the traits Emma attributes to Mark (King of Pentacles) and the emotional depth of Mark's feelings for Emma (the Lovers).

Below the Significator cards, in positions 6 and 7, we consider the foundation from which each of them tends to operate. This card can reveal what Emma and Mark require from a relationship to feel safe, secure, and grounded. Beneath Emma we find the Knight of Swords. For her, it is important that she and Mark communicate on a deep level, and that he has the ability to openly express his feelings and sentiments to her. Affection is also important to Mark's foundation, indicated by the Ten of Cups. This card confirms that Mark feels he has found the woman of his dreams.

Emotionally, they both require validation and expression in their relationship. Considering the cards we have already seen in this reading, there is no reason to doubt that both are willing to share with the other, openly and often.

Spiritually, Mark will be more verbal in expressing his feelings and hopes for the future, as indicated by the Ten of Cups. He is intent on marrying Emma and building a happy life with her. As an earth sign, Emma may operate on a more practical level. The Knight of Swords in this position indicates she is more in tune with her thoughts than her emotions. Emma must learn to accept what might appear to be neediness on Mark's part and reassure him when he feels hesitant. Likewise, Mark should balance his emotions with practicality. If both of them give the relationship loving mindfulness, it should proceed smoothly.

As representatives of the future, the final three cards promise a positive road ahead. The Empress indicates that Mark and Emma are content in the relationship, and that they will soon reach a new level of communication and commitment (Ace of Swords).

The Two of Wands foretells a proposal between them, either an invitation from Mark to move in together or perhaps marriage.

Emotionally, the Empress suggests that Emma and Mark will continue to nurture each other and the relationship. The Ace of Swords indicates that they can enhance their feelings and commitments by expanding their levels of communication. They will be inspired to take their partnership to the next level, represented by the Two of Wands as an invitation or proposal to join forces.

Spiritually, these three cards show continued advancement in the relationship. The Empress represents fertility and infuses this connection with great potential for spiritual growth and, quite possibly, children. The Ace of Swords speaks of an important victory, and assures Mark and Emma that their relationship has the power to succeed. A spiritual proposal is in their future, as indicated by the Two of Wands.

Linda and Taylor's Business Partnership Reading

Linda is interested in forming a partnership with Taylor, her mentor in the field of metaphysics. She feels that together, they could establish a successful and profitable business. We chose the Queen of Wands as Linda's significator, as she is an Aries. For Taylor, we chose the High Priestess, reflective of the psychic and intuitive work she does.

These were the cards that appeared in the reading:

Significator 1—Queen of Wands
Significator 2—High Priestess
Three of Cups
Two of Wands
Ten of Pentacles
Ace of Wands
Queen of Cups
Wheel of Fortune
Eight of Pentacles
Six of Swords
Nine of Pentacles
The Fool

The Three of Cups located in position 1 indicates mutual affection between Linda and Taylor, and that, spiritually, they uplift and inspire each other. Because of the creative energy that flows between them, this bodes well for any work they do together, and may be the reason Linda thought of the idea to merge their mutual gifts into a business venture.

In position 2 we find the Two of Wands, a card that can signify a business proposal. Located behind Linda, it confirms that what is moving her toward Taylor is the idea that they should work together. The Ten of Pentacles occupies the number 3 position, and reveals why Taylor would be interested in this partnership. What makes Taylor open to this idea is the potential to take her work to the next level, and to boost her income.

Relationship Reading
Linda and Taylor's Business Partnership

Viewing the cards in this row as a group, we see validation that Linda's idea to form a business partnership is supported by Spirit, as indicated by the Two of Wands, the Queen of Wands (representing business, inspiration, and spirituality) and the Three of Cups. The type of business she wants to form is based on a desire to build her own metaphysical skills, and to promote the gifts her friend already possesses (High Priestess and Ten of Pentacles).

Emotionally, both Linda and Taylor like this idea, though they have different goals for the partnership. Linda feels that this business would support her desire to do more spiritual work, taking her out of her current, mundane career. Taylor, who loves her work but often struggles financially, sees this as a way to build more security and reputation.

Spiritually, the two wand cards that appear in this reading suggest this idea was inspired by the Divine, and, based on the Three of Cups located in the middle, has the potential to fulfill each of their needs. This card promises a joyful partnership, and reflects their ability to work together in harmonious and balanced ways. The Ten of Pentacles suggests a strong foundation in the partnership, while the High Priestess identifies their potential partnership as being intuitively based and divinely supported.

The Ace of Wands appears in position 4, located above Linda's significator. Her mind is filled with endless ideas on how to build, market, and promote this new business. Aces represent new beginnings, while wands represent creative expression, assertive action, and determination. Above Taylor, in position five, we see the Queen of Cups. This card indicates that Taylor is open to sharing her gifts, wants to bring them out into the world more, and feels that a partnership with Linda would be supportive, loving, and prosperous.

Emotionally, both feel the need to expand, but in different ways. Both are willing to combine their gifts, in the hopes of creating new and more fulfilling careers.

Spiritually, both Linda and Taylor are intrigued by this idea's potential. They are prepared to make a leap of faith, invest time and effort into the business, and rely on the Universe to help take them where they want to go.

The Wheel of Fortune sits below Linda in position 6, and represents the foundation of her idea. Karmically, she believes that this is the way out of her drudgery and into a more fulfilling career. Anything could happen with the Wheel of Fortune positioned here, but in an effort to advance, Linda is ready to weather the ups and downs of this business venture. With the Eight of Pentacles located beneath Taylor, we see that she is skilled in her work, and possesses the professional knowledge, background, and ability to make this business a success. With this card located in the foundation position, she is hoping to expand her career, rather than change it.

Emotionally, the Wheel of Fortune indicates taking risks, which Linda is prepared to do. For Taylor, the Eight of Wands portrays the confidence and well-being that could come from reaching a pinnacle of success in her field.

Spiritually, the Wheel of Fortune, as a major arcana card, suggests that Linda is ready to take a leap of faith, turn her back on a stable but unfulfilling career, and let the Universe open a brand new world to her. For Taylor, who has always had the support of Spirit in her work, it suggests the idea that karmically, the Universe is ready to take her to the next level in her development.

The first steps to establishing this business are outlined in the final three cards. In positions 8, 9, and 10, we have the Six of Swords, the Nine of Pentacles, and the Fool. The Six of Swords indicates that Linda and Taylor need to combine their ideas and formulate a plan. Swords represent ideas, and the sixth card of this suit illustrates a process that one is midway through completing. These two must meet halfway and decide which responsibilities each will take on in the business. The Nine of Pentacles addresses their need for financial capital: How will Linda and Taylor gather the funds to get their new venture off the ground? Once these two issues are addressed, the Fool promises that they will be able to get their new business up and running.

Emotionally, Linda and Taylor have to identify the strengths and talents each will bring to the partnership. With the Six of Swords present, they may discover conflicts that need to be addressed. Taylor may be unable to contribute to the financial end of the business, which could create some concern, although the presence of the Nine of Pentacles suggests that the money they need will come through spiritual means. The excitement and inspiration of starting their own business, full of potential and dreams, is evident in the final card, the Fool.

Spiritually, they must be patient, and willing to move in a linear and disciplined way to create this business. They will have to align their progress with Universal timing and keep their goal in sight at all times, based on the image in the Six of Swords. Linda and Taylor trust that the money they need will come, and quite expect it to appear magically, thanks to the intervention of Spirit (Nine of Pentacles). The Fool card encourages them to move forward with the business partnership, and though there are aspects of the unknown ahead, Linda and Taylor are spiritually inspired and ready to take a leap of faith in this direction.

Dominique's Miracle Baby Reading

After ten years of trying to conceive, without success, Dominique paid a visit to a fertility specialist, where she discovered that her chances of becoming pregnant were very slim. After hearing this news, she decided that it was time to let go of her dream. Soon after, when she least expected it, she became pregnant. Though her child is not yet born, she would like to know about the special bond she and this miracle baby have.

We chose the Empress card, which represents motherhood, as Dominique's significator. We then decided that the Sun should represent the unborn child, based on this card's joyful image of an infant riding a horse.

Here are the cards that came up:

>   Significator 1—The Empress
>   Significator 2—The Sun
>   The World
>   Seven of Swords
>   Eight of Pentacles
>   Two of Pentacles
>   Knight of Cups
>   Ace of Swords
>   The Hierophant
>   The Moon
>   Eight of Wands
>   Three of Cups

Between Dominique and her unborn child we find the World. As a major arcana card, the message is powerful. The union between her and her miracle baby will change Dominique's life. The World card embodies the idea of attainment and fulfillment. Because it touches on the concepts of accomplishment, higher education, global travel, and completion, we can see that as a mother, Dominique will be instrumental to the child's development. This card also indicates that her child has much to teach Dominique as well. They will share a lifetime of experiences neither

Relationship Reading
Dominique's Miracle Baby

could have had without the other, making this one of the most significant relationships the two of them will have. Spiritually, the World tells us that the Universe knows our dreams and supports them, even when it seems our desires are out of our reach. In essence, this card speaks to the power of Spirit, through whom all things are possible.

In the number two position behind Dominique, we find the Seven of Swords. In this situation, there was no reason to expect a child, as she had been told that her dream of having a child was next to impossible. She felt that this opportunity had been stolen from her. Behind the baby, in the number 3 position, lays the Eight of Pentacles. This card speaks to the patient waiting and physical development Dominique will experience during the pregnancy. Apprised of eight pentacles, or eight months, we find that, numerologically, this aligns closely with the usual nine-month cycle of pregnancy.

Reviewing this row of cards as a whole, we see that Dominique felt she was going to be deprived of motherhood (Seven of Swords and the Empress), but that her world (the World) changed when she discovered she was pregnant. The Eight of Pentacles reflects the pregnancy in progress.

Emotionally, she was devastated by the diagnosis that she could not have children, one of her greatest desires (the World). The Sun reflects the joy that welled up within her when she found out that she was, indeed, with child.

Spiritually, these cards speak to the concept that when we accept disappointment, Spirit can turn things around and bring our heart's desires into being, in the most miraculous of ways.

In position 4, we find the Two of Pentacles. Situated above the Empress, this card portrays Dominique as one who is able to maintain her balance. As she awaits the arrival of her child, she will consider what needs to be done, and how to prepare in the most effective way possible. Over the baby's head in position 5 we find the Knight of Cups. This card represents a pure form of love. The messages the baby sends her, through an expanding body and a kick here and there, tell her that he is near. This card can also reflect the infant's presence in the womb. (Cups represent the element of water.)

Emotionally, these two cards indicate balance and messages of love, and reflect that both parties are preparing for the day they will meet face to face.

Spiritually, aware that her dream is about to come true, Dominique is able to move beyond disappointment and view her life in a more balanced manner (Two of Pentacles). The baby represents the very essence of spiritual love, as he is a gift from the heavens.

Beneath the Empress, in position 6, we find the Ace of Swords, indicating that Dominique's foundation is strong and empowered. With thoughts of the impending birth to direct her actions, she is on solid footing. With the Ace of Swords in this position, an epidural incision or a Caesarean delivery could be indicated. The Hierophant in position 7 below the baby, basically promises a problem-free pregnancy and normal birth. Since the Hierophant represents tradition and rules, its presence implies that, as long as Dominique takes care of herself, the pregnancy should proceed without incident or concern.

Emotionally, the Ace of Swords represents Dominique's sense of inspiration and hope. It implies that she will experience more energy and optimism. The Hierophant speaks to a happy and healthy baby with an even temperament, though he may become demanding or fussy if his basic needs are not met immediately.

Spiritually, the Ace of Swords—in this deck, a hand with a victorious sword emerging from the clouds—affirms that her pregnancy is a gift from the heavens. The Hierophant reminds her that nothing is impossible when Spirit intervenes.

The final three cards in this layout are the Moon, the Eight of Wands, and the Three of Cups. The Moon represents the pregnancy itself, while the Eight of Wands could imply that the baby will arrive early, possibly two days or two weeks before the due date. Because we saw a shortened pregnancy cycle in the Eight of Pentacles to the right of the baby, as well as a hint that a Caesarean delivery might be necessary, we can surmise that the baby may come early. The Three of Cups predicts that there will be much celebration surrounding this little one's arrival.

Emotionally, the Moon represents the speculation Dominique will experience as she wonders and waits for her child to arrive. Before she knows it (Eight of Wands), she will give birth to a new life, and be overcome with a joy greater than she can imagine (Three of Cups).

Spiritually, the Moon represents a time of incubation, intuition, and psychic expansion. Dominique will begin to experience the supernatural ties between mother and child long before she gives birth. When the baby arrives (Eight of Wands), Dominique will be transported to a new place of awareness and enlightenment, ready to embrace this child on all levels. Because Dominique knows that this baby is a miracle, the celebration of his birth will be even more profound and precious to her (Three of Cups).

DECISION TREES READING

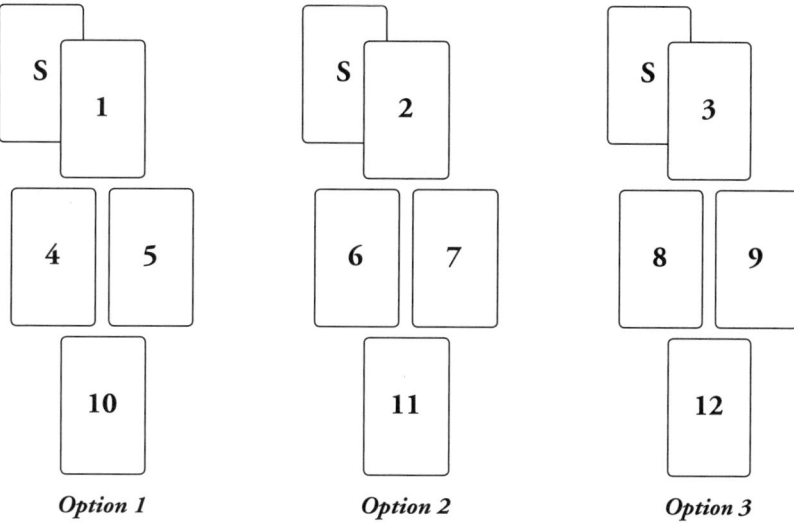

Option 1   Option 2   Option 3

The Decision Trees reading is designed to clarify your options when two or more choices are on the table. By gathering additional insights through this reading, you will be guided to make the most informed decision possible.

The examples in this section consider three choices, but can be modified to review two, four, or more options. Simply lay out an additional tree for each possible choice. Each four-card layout describes a specific option that can first be read individually, and then as a whole in combination with the alternate choices about which you are asking.

Directions: Choose a significator card (see significator tables in Appendix B) to represent each choice or option. (As an example, if you are making a choice between three likely candidates for a job, you would choose a different significator for each of the prospective employees.) Place the significators at the top of your table. Shuffle the remaining cards and lay them out from left to right, as indicated.

Cards 1, 2, and 3 represent an initial overview or important information regarding each of your options.

Cards 4 and 5 refer to option or decision tree one, cards 6 and 7 to option two, and cards 8 and 9 to option three. (See the illustrations in each example.) This second grouping of cards reveals the consequence of one's choice. Hidden influences, traits, or conditions may also appear here.

Cards 10, 11, and 12 outline the likely outcome of each choice. At this point in the reading, you will consider what is known (through discussions with your querent or information you have already gathered), your intuition, and the messages contained in the cards, all of which will be factored together for a final analysis.

The best way to determine the potential of each option is to interpret the cards in each tree as a group, moving to the next tree, reading it as a whole, and finally, exploring the cards that appear in option three. Once you have reviewed all options, a clear choice should emerge.

Joshua's New Assistant Reading

Joshua needs to hire a new assistant. He has interviewed a number of candidates, three of whom appear ideal for the job. He is uncertain which applicant would best fill the position. He began by selecting three Significator cards to represent each potential assistant. Through their resumes, Joshua has access to their birth dates, and selected the following cards: Richard is an Aries, represented by the King of Wands, while James, a Pisces, is represented by the King of Cups. Because Karren is a Gemini, her significator is the Queen of Swords.

The following cards were pulled for each decision tree option. To begin, we will take a look at these trees individually to see what each candidate can bring to the position.

> Option One:
> James, significator—King of Wands

The cards drawn for James' tree were:

> Page/Knave of Wands
> Two of Wands
> Seven of Pentacles
> Queen of Wands

Located in position 1, the Page/Knave of Wands identifies James as a person who is inspired, creative, and hard-working. He possesses the ability to take direction and practice follow-through. On the downside, he may be overly ambitious or argumentative, traits often assigned to this court card. Spiritually, James embodies the passion, drive, and fearlessness that will make him a valued employee.

In positions 4 and 5 of this tree we have the Two of Wands and the Seven of Pentacles. The Two of Wands implies that Joshua has already been tempted to offer the job to James. It suggests a good decision, while the Seven of Pentacles affirms that James will work hard and make this job his priority. He will not mind working overtime, and will give as well as he gets. If this position requires it, James can build the company's clientele and bring in new business.

           Option 1   Option 2   Option 3
                    Decision Trees Reading
                    Joshua's New Assistant

Interestingly enough, we find yet another wand, the queen, in position 10, the final card in this tree. Notice that four of the five cards (including the significator) in this tree are wands. This speaks well of the candidate as an employee, (wands refer to business), and to his creativity, endurance, and enthusiasm. Spiritually, the Queen of Wands represents one who is faithful to his or her commitments, true to him- or herself, and intuitively aware.

Because we are looking for traits and character in this reading, we read this court card representative of what Joshua will gain if he hires this man. The Queen of Wands carries the reputation of being assertive, creative, determined, and frugal. She does not waste money or time, and carries an intuitive brilliance. James embodies these traits and, at this point, appears to be the stand-out candidate for this job.

Option Two:
Richard, significator—King of Cups

The cards drawn for Richard were:

Eight of Cups
Five of Pentacles
Three of Wands
Eight of Swords

The Eight of Cups in position 2 reveals that Richard is ready to leave the past behind and try his hand at new things. Though he has less experience than James, he is hoping for a chance to prove himself. Emotionally, he has processed and dealt with issues that may have limited his work efforts in the past and, of the three candidates, may be the only one who is not currently employed. This could make him appear anxious or overly eager. Spiritually, he has just finished an important personal transformation, and is now attempting to reclaim some level of stability and security.

In positions 6 and 7, the next cards in this option, we have the Five of Pentacles and the Three of Wands. There appears to be an air of sorrow or disappointment around this candidate that could interfere with his ability to do consistent work. It may even be a sign of depression. The Three of Wands warns that he is not a self-starter, and will require much direction. He may be the type of employee who waits for someone to tell him what to do, rather than being self-directed. Spiritually, the Five of Pentacles cautions that he may still be working through past emotions, which may interfere with his work. The Three of Wands indicates one who waits for direction from a higher authority, and in this job, that could prove a detriment.

The final card for this choice, in position 11, is the Eight of Swords. This man does not know what he is getting into, and seems unaware that he is not suited for this job. Because we see him as unemployed, he may simply be interviewing for any job openings he finds. Spiritually, he seems to be drifting along and fairly self-focused. Spiritually, the Eight of Swords suggests one who is unaware of how his actions are affecting others, and trapped by limited ideas. If Joshua hires Richard, he might find himself frustrated by this candidate's lack of conviction, experience, and drive.

Option Three:
Karren, significator—Queen of Swords

The cards that came up for Karren were:

Ten of Cups
Seven of Cups
Seven of Wands
Ten of Pentacles

The Ten of Cups in position 3 identifies Karren as a well-rounded person, capable of performing many different tasks. Depending on what type of assistant position Joshua is offering, this multi-tasking candidate might just fit the bill. Emotionally, Karren is good with people, so if this position involves socializing or working with the public, she will do well. However, this card also suggests that she may be prone to office gossip and mood swings, making it difficult for her to work under pressure. Spiritually, the Ten of Cups indicates that Karren is intuitive, aware, and empathetic, which may or may not be important in this job.

Cards 8 and 9 are the Seven of Cups and Seven of Wands. Karren appears to have a lot on her mind, and could find it difficult to remain focused on the task at hand (Seven of Cups). If she is unable to complete a project on time or misses work due to a crisis of one kind or another, she will try to defend her actions and argue her point, rather than correcting the problem (Seven of Wands). Note that both cards are Sevens, implying that the emotional partnerships in her life (friends, lovers, family) could prevent Karren from making work a priority. Spiritually, the Seven of Cups represents someone who is easily overwhelmed, while the Seven of Wands indicates someone who is often on the defensive. These cards can suggest someone who is lacking balance and may have a difficult time seeing reality.

The last card in this tree option, position 12, is the Ten of Pentacles. This card implies that Karren is focused on the salary she will earn, and that it will not be long before she asks Joshua for a raise. She may appear able to handle a number of tasks at once, but, with too many balls in the air (note the image on this card, a man standing with a handful of balls), she is more than likely to drop a few of them in the process. There is a sense that Karren is emotionally immature, prone to socializing and doing less and less work as time goes on. Spiritually, this card reveals that her physical world holds priority over her spiritual development, and that her focus is weighed down by her ego and material desires. If Joshua hires this candidate, he could find her spending her time around the water cooler gossiping when she should be working.

Reviewing these three candidates overall, James stands out as the right candidate for this job, making him the clear choice for Joshua's assistant.

Zachary's Dating Life Reading

Zachary is dating three women. Though he enjoys the company of all three, at this time Zachary would like to focus on only one woman, to see where the relationship will go. He is not sure of these women's birth dates, so, to make each girl easy to identify, Zachary looks through the tarot deck for images that resemble each of these women to use as their significators. (See appendix B for more information on choosing a significator when birth dates are unavailable.)

For Kaye, a blonde veterinarian, he selects the Strength card. Shawne is a brunette and loves to garden, so for her, he opts for the Nine of Pentacles. Regarding Tina, a redhead with two small children, he chooses the Empress.

>Option one:
>Kaye, significator—Strength

For this option, the following cards came up:

>Four of Cups
>Three of Wands
>Three of Pentacles
>Four of Pentacles

The Four of Cups in position 1 indicates that Zachary has grown bored (one interpretation of this card) with Kaye. Emotionally, the man in the picture is looking away from the cups in front of him, searching for something more inspiring. Spiritually, he is watching the heavens for a sign, direction, or inspiration.

In the second group of cards, we find two cards with the number three. This could indicate that Kaye is one of three, with no traits that stand out from the rest. The Three of Wands represents someone who is standing back, waiting for guidance, or, as depicted in this card, waiting for their "ship to come in," while the Three of Pentacles displays a man holding one of three shields. This could be interpreted as taking one of the shields down (or choices out of the mix). Neither of these cards reveal any emotional attachment to Kaye on Zachary's part, nor any spiritual inspiration.

Option 1　　　　*Option 2*　　　　*Option 3*

Decision Trees Reading
Zachary's Dating Life

The final card, the Four of Pentacles, shows Zachary pulling back from this situation. He does not feel emotionally invested in Kaye. When one person stands back from another, it cuts off the spiritual energy between them, so Kaye appears to be one option he can eliminate right away.

Option two:
    Shawne, significator—Nine of Pentacles

The cards that were drawn for Shawne were:

The Fool
The Sun
The Magician
The Wheel of Fortune

Here we have four major arcana cards, dictating that Zachary pay close attention to this option. The Fool speaks to a new journey, aligning with Zachary's question regarding which girl he should focus his attentions on. Emotionally, becoming exclusive with Shawne would bring a fresh view to his world and has the potential to become a long-term partner. Spiritually, because of the high number of major arcana, there is power in this relationship not evident in option one, Kaye.

The Sun and the Magician, both positive and encouraging cards, occupy the second row of this option. The Sun is one of two major arcana cards that suggest a happy and loving relationship, while the Magician indicates the powerful attraction that exists between Zachary and Shawne. Emotionally, these cards represent the passion, energy, and magic that reside in this connection. Spiritually, the cards support the idea of building a relationship with her, as the Sun represents life-giving energy while the Magician implies a karmic connection.

The Wheel of Fortune in the final position encourages Zachary to take a chance with Shawne. In fact, with four major arcana cards in this tree, he would be foolish not to. Though there may have been emotional ups and downs in the past, making this relationship exclusive would stabilize them both. Spiritually, this card represents karma, and suggests that the Universe will be on his side if he chooses this option.

>Option three:
>Tina, significator—the Empress

The following cards were drawn for Tina:

>Five of Cups
>Two of Wands
>Nine of Wands
>Seven of Cups

The Five of Cups in the first position does not bode well for this option. Tina may be overly emotional, and perhaps, already too attached to Zachary. Even though it has been casual up to this point, she may exhibit signs of neediness or mood swings and make it difficult for Zachary to end this relationship. Spiritually, this card suggests that better relationship options lay ahead for both of them, once he ends the connection.

The Two and Nine of Wands in the second row indicate that it is time for Zachary to make a decision, along with a warning that he will have to erect strong boundaries to enforce it. Again, we have a clue that it may be difficult for Tina to let go. Emotionally, there has been some passion between them, but Zachary is looking for more in a relationship, and needs to stand his ground. Spiritually, the Two of Wands, depicting one path separating into two, illustrates a parting of ways.

With the Seven of Cups completing this tree, it is clear that if he were to choose Tina, many worries would accompany this relationship. The emotional heaviness that surrounds Tina would soon make Zachary weary, and he would have to withdraw. Spiritually, the Seven of Cups suggests that, while Tina has many of the qualities Zachary desires in a long-term relationship, her emotional instability would make it difficult for them to maintain.

Looking over the three options or trees as a whole, Shawne stands out as the ideal choice for Zachary to pursue an exclusive relationship with.

Mary Ellen's Anniversary Gift Reading

Mary Ellen is looking for a special gift for her parents' fiftieth wedding anniversary. She is considering three options, and cannot decide between them. She looks carefully through the cards to select an appropriate significator for each potential gift. (See appendix B for more information on choosing significators.) She is considering a pair of antique silver candlesticks her mother admires, so for this choice, she selects the Two of Wands (two representing a pair, wands representing the element of fire or candles). She is also aware that her parents need a new television set. For this option, Mary Ellen chooses the Wheel of Fortune, which represents one of her parents' favorite television shows. She can also go in with her brothers and sisters to buy them a Caribbean cruise. For this option, she chooses the Sun, reflective of the climate they would experience on the cruise.

Option One:
Antique silver candlesticks, significator—Two of Wands

For this gift choice, the following cards were drawn:

The Emperor
Five of Cups
Seven of Swords
Temperance

It is clear to see from these cards that if Mary Ellen chooses the candlesticks her mother admires, her father will feel left out (Emperor). Emotionally, she needs to opt for a gift that both parents will appreciate, and this card reminds her to consider her father's feelings in the process. Spiritually, these cards suggest finding a gift that will suit both her parents.

The Five of Cups displays someone who is sad, while the Seven of Swords implies that her father may feel cheated if Mary Ellen's gift is geared more towards her mother. Emotionally, this card suggests that her father will be disappointed, which is not her goal. Spiritually, the cards are warning her to stay away from a one-sided gift.

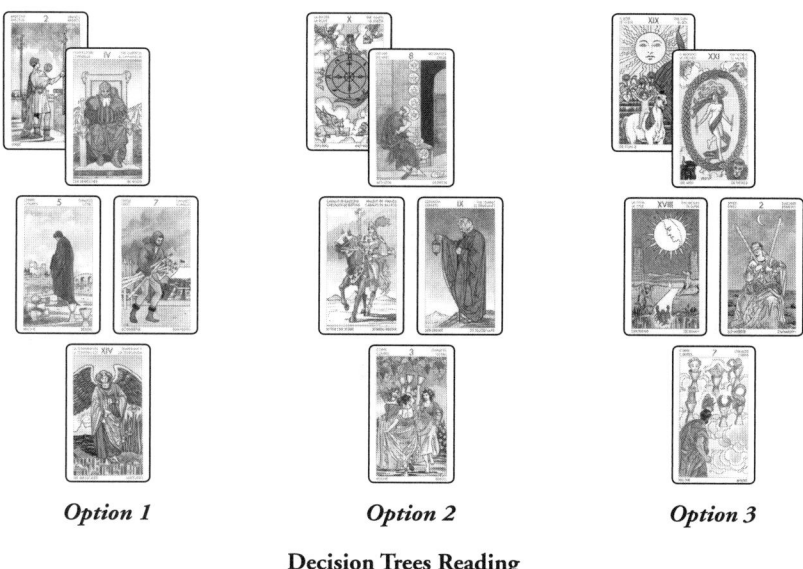

Option 1 *Option 2* *Option 3*

Decision Trees Reading
Mary Ellen's Anniversary Gift

Though the candlesticks are a good idea in general, the Temperance card says Mary Ellen must consider both parties in her selection. Emotionally, this card represents balance and fairness, as illustrated by the angel pouring water from one cup to another. Spiritually, though her intentions are good, Mary Ellen is being asked to reconsider this option and look for a more equitable gift.

Option two:
   Television set, significator—Wheel of Fortune

For this option, the following cards were drawn:

Eight of Pentacles
Knight of Wands
The Hermit
Three of Cups

INTERMEDIATE READINGS | 125

In this position, the Eight of Pentacles refers to a gift that will keep giving for years to come. Because her parents watch TV daily, a television seems a good gift, though it will cost her more (pentacles) than the candlesticks. Emotionally, it will provide both her parents and Mary Ellen a sense of satisfaction, as the television set they now own is on its last legs. Spiritually, this card speaks to picking a gift that she knows both of them need and will use regularly.

The Knight of Wands and the Hermit appear in the second group of cards. The Knight of Wands affirms that the television is an inspired idea, while the Hermit reminds Mary Ellen that her parents are not as mobile as they once were. Emotionally, these two cards indicate that television is a main form of entertainment for them. Spiritually, the Knight of Wands encourages her to act on this idea, while the Hermit compels her to begin researching her options for the ideal television set.

The Three of Cups indicates that this gift would be appreciated by both her parents, and that Mary Ellen can feel confident in this choice. Emotionally, a new television will bring them both much happiness. Spiritually, it affirms the simple joys inherent in such a thoughtful and useful gift.

> Option three:
> Caribbean cruise, significator—The Sun

The cards drawn for this option were:

The World
The Moon
Two of Swords
Seven of Cups

As the most expensive gift option in this reading, the Caribbean cruise is represented by the World in the first position. The World can indicate travel, and, as a major arcana card, might seem a positive choice. Mary Ellen's parents do not travel often, and the cruise would give them the opportunity to see a part of the world they have never seen. Emotionally, it might represent a second honeymoon for them, which is in tune with the occasion, their fiftieth wedding anniversary. At first glance, the gift appears to be spiritually inspired.

However, the Moon and Two of Swords in the next row give pause to the idea. They imply that there would be some hesitation on the part of Mary Ellen's parents. Though Mary Ellen and her siblings see this as a grand gesture, their parents may feel uncertain about taking such a trip (Two of Swords). Spiritually, these cards suggest that this option might create more concern for her parents than Mary Ellen and her siblings realize (the Moon).

The Seven of Cups in the final position suggests additional worries. Emotionally, her parents may panic when faced with the idea of traveling outside of the country. They could become overly concerned with the details: how will they get there, who will take care of the houseplants, will they need passports, and so on. Spiritually, this would create unnecessary conflicts within her parents. Mary Ellen's parents may also worry that, since their children spent so much money on the cruise, they must accept it, even if they are not keen on the idea. Taking the trip might present challenges they are not up to physically, mentally, or emotionally.

Based on these cards, Mary Ellen's safest bet is to go with the television. This is a gift she knows both her parents will appreciate, and one that will give them pleasure on a daily basis.

THE VEIL/TRUTH READING

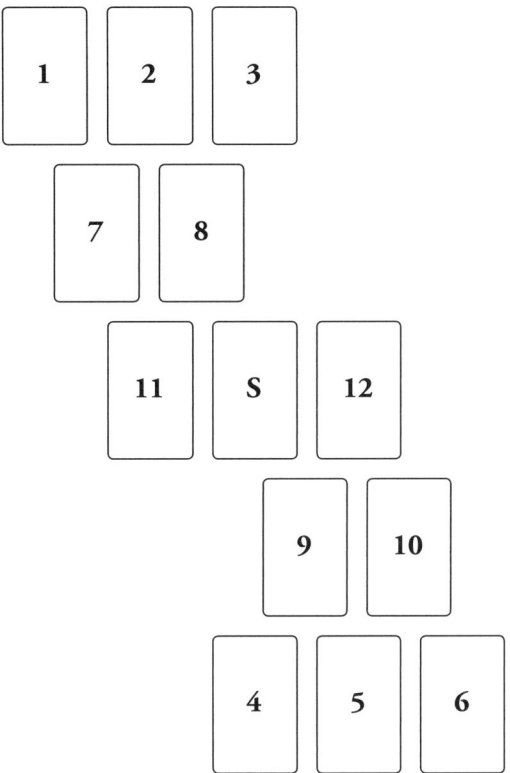

This reading is designed to remove the "veil" from a situation and reveal the truth. Oftentimes we can see only one side of a conflict, or would like to know what lies beneath the surface of an event. In the Veil/Truth reading, we can expand our understanding of a situation to discover, for example, if someone is lying to us, or, if we may be lying to ourselves. This reading can also be helpful when one is having trouble understanding or accepting another's decision. The cards, as shown in the examples, are laid out to illustrate the old adage that, "The truth lies somewhere in the middle."

Directions: Shuffle the cards and lay them out as shown in the illustrations. In the middle, place a significator card to represent the person or situation you would like to know more about. (See significator tables in appendix B for more information.) Cards 11 and 12, the truth cards, should line up on either side of the Significator when you are finished setting up the layout.

Cards 1, 2, and 3 will represent the truth as the querent sees it, or what the facts appear to be on the surface.

Cards 4, 5, and 6, at the bottom of the layout, will represent the truth as the other party involved sees it, or what the facts are about this particular situation.

Cards 7 and 8 represent the veil that hangs over the situation, usually actions by the other party that are creating illusion or confusion for the querent. This row will often verify that the person's words and deeds are not in alignment, to the querent's way of thinking.

Cards 9 and 10 represent what the querent does not know or cannot control about the facts, behavior, or decisions made by the other party.

Cards 11 and 12 represent the truth or the heart of the matter. These cards sit on either side of the Significator, and identify the actual facts regarding the situation.

(Concept/Design: Louise Gilbertson)

Dan's Well-Being Reading

Phyllis suspects that her teenaged son Dan has become friends with a group of troubled boys at school, and may be involved in illegal activities, namely drugs. He has become distant and withdrawn. Initially, she attributed his behavior to puberty, but she wants to be sure nothing else is going on. Phyllis chose the Knight of Swords for Dan's significator and placed it in the center, based on the fact that he is an Aquarius under the age of 21 (knights represent persons between the age of 14 and 20).

For the top row of cards she drew:

> The Empress
> Three of Wands
> Five of Pentacles

Cards 1, 2, and 3 confirm Phyllis' suspicions. As the mother (the Empress) she has stood back and watched (Three of Wands) trying to determine what is going on with Dan. Emotionally, she feels shut out and cannot seem to get any information from him, as indicated by the Five of Pentacles. Spiritually and intuitively, she is worried about his welfare and state of mind.

For the bottom row (Dan's truth) we drew:

> King of Swords
> The Fool
> Two of Wands

In cards 4, 5, and 6 we see what Dan is experiencing. The King of Swords, a more mature version of Dan, suggests that emotionally, he has decided he is a man and can make his own decisions. He no longer looks to his mother for direction and advice. The Fool implies that he has embarked on a new journey, and could be moving with crowds she would not approve of. The Two of Wands indicates that he has made a decision to follow a different path. Spiritually, he is making choices that reflect a desire to move independently, unconcerned about what might lie ahead, also represented by the Fool.

The Veil/Truth Reading
Dan's Well-Being

In row two we have:

Queen of Pentacles
Page/Knave of Swords

Because Phyllis is a Virgo, the Queen of Pentacles in position 7 represents her. The Page/Knave of Swords in position 8 reveals that Dan is looking in a different direction for inspiration and validation. Notice that in these two cards, the people have turned away from each other. The son has turned away from the mother, and neither can see what the other is doing. Emotionally, these cards represent a distance growing between them, and a disconnect on a spiritual level.

In row four, we see:

King of Wands
Seven of Cups

These cards confirm what we observed earlier in the reading, that Dan feels he is a man and can make his own decisions (King of Wands in position 9). The Seven of Cups, in position 10, is often an indicator of addictive or illusion-filled behavior, and can represent a multitude of medications in some health readings. This is the first definitive sign that Dan may, indeed, be involved with drugs, or moving in that direction. Emotionally, he may feel overwhelmed or under pressure to go along with the new crowd he is involved with (Seven of Cups) and refuses to back down on his decision to make his own choices (King of Wands). Spiritually, the Seven of Cups can represent a disconnect from his inner truths, while the King of Wands portrays a headstrong attitude.

The middle row of cards contain:

Five of Wands
Ten of Pentacles

The Five of Wands, to the left of Dan's significator (position 11), and the Ten of Pentacles to his right (position 12), tell us what is actually going on. In this deck, the image of matches on the card strongly suggests that Dan is, in fact, "playing with fire." The Ten of Pentacles displays a man with a handful of round objects that could, in this reading, indicate someone who has been offering Dan drugs.

Emotionally, there are many indicators in this reading that affirm Phyllis' fears. Dan has pulled back and shut her out. Though this can be typical during teenage years, there appears to be more to Dan's behavior. He feels defiant, and wants to make his own decisions, based on the three kings who appear on his side of the reading.

Spiritually, this reading is alerting Phyllis that it is time to take action and intervene in Dan's activities and friendships. If she does not, Dan could move deeper and deeper into situations for which he is neither prepared for, nor mature enough to handle.

Louise's Marriage Reading

Louise suspects that her husband Steve is having an online affair. He is spending hours on the Internet and, recently, went away suddenly for the weekend to "go fishing with his brother." She wants to know if anything is going on, and if her marriage is in trouble.

Steve is a Leo, so she selected the King of Wands as the Significator for this reading, and placed it in the center.

She then pulled the following cards for the top row:

>Five of Wands
>Nine of Swords
>The Star

Cards 1, 2, and 3 of this layout speak to Louise's suspicions. The Five of Wands confirms the emotional struggles she is experiencing, and her sense that she is in competition for her husband's affections. The Nine of Swords indicates that blocks to communication have risen up around them. The Star supports her belief that he is immersed in some type of Internet intrigue. Emotionally, these cards reflect her sense that there is trouble brewing, and that her most important relationship (the Star) is in jeopardy. Spiritually, these cards are encouraging her to trust her intuition and find a way to address her suspicions.

For row five she drew:

>Four of Cups
>Queen of Swords
>Nine of Pentacles

The bottom row, cards 4, 5, and 6, outline Steve's reality. The Four of Cups implies that Steve has grown bored, and quite possibly, has found someone new to inspire his imagination. Louise is a Scorpio, so the Queen of Swords would indicate the other woman. This card is describing someone well-versed in the art of conversation. Swords can also represent electronic forms of communication, such as the Internet. Next is the Nine of Pentacles. This card illustrates a multitude of exchanges

The Veil/Truth Reading
Louise's Marriage

between Steve and the other woman. In this case, the many pentacles surrounding the woman could indicate a stockpile of e-mails or instant messages.

In row two, we see:

Five of Pentacles
Eight of Cups

Cards 7 and 8 reveal facts Louise may be unaware of, and in this case, speak to Steve's search for something more in his life. Again, the Five of Pentacles may suggest that he feels left out, or that he senses that something is missing in his life. The Eight of Cups implies that Steve is searching beyond his family for affirmation.

Physically unable to move out of his rut (Five of Pentacles), Steve has found a way to reawaken his emotions (Eight of Cups). Spiritually, the Eight of Cups implies that because Steve neither knows how or wants to change his circumstances, he's looking for a distraction to ease his frustration.

These cards were drawn for row three:

Page/Knave of Wands
Knight of Wands

Cards 9 and 10 represent things over which Louise has no control. When Steve speaks with this woman, he feels inspired (Page/Knave of Wands) and more masculine (Knight of Wands). Emotionally, he is seeking validation from a stranger who appears to see him in a different light. Spiritually, he is living in a fantasy world in an effort to forget the reality of his life. The Page and Knight of Wands speak to ego-based actions filled with passion, but no real emotion.

For the center row, we have:

Page/Knave of Pentacles
Queen of Cups

In the middle row, we arrive at the heart of the matter. To Steve's left (in position 11) is the Page of Pentacles. This card reveals that, even though he is engaging in flirtations over the Internet, Steve has no intention of leaving his marriage, and is fairly content with Louise. Louise, as a Scorpio, is represented by the Queen of Cups in position 12. His interactions online have nothing to do with her, but are created solely to soothe his ego.

Emotionally, this is a difficult situation for Louise. Though the reading implies that this is a passing phase, she may decide to confront Steve and ask him to be honest about his activities, or she may pull back emotionally from the relationship.

Spiritually, this reading affirms to Louise that there is a problem with Steve. Because it is still in its initial stages, and there are no cards in the reading to indicate that Steve and the other woman have been in contact with each other in real life, there is a chance that Louise and Steve can use this incident to reopen the doors of communication between them. As long as Steve continues to hide from reality, there can be no real change in the relationship. Louise may suggest couple therapy to help them reestablish their connection and commitment. In doing so, Steve can stop denying his unhappiness, and do something about it by making personal changes, rather than bringing harm to his marriage.

Donald's Employee Issue Reading

Donald suspects that one of his employees is stealing from his company. Though he has no proof, he has narrowed it down to a technician named Ron, whom he has observed behaving in secretive and unsocial ways. Before he confronts Ron, Donald wants more information to validate his suspicions. He knows that Ron's birthday is sometime in July, so he chooses the King of Cups for the significator, placing it in the center of the layout.

These are these cards he drew for row one:

> The Hermit
> Three of Cups
> Seven of Swords

The cards in positions 1, 2, and 3 define Donald's perception of the situation. The Hermit illustrates someone searching for something, possibly during a party or meeting (implied by the Three of Cups), only to discover it missing (Seven of Swords). Because Donald could not find supplies he was looking for during a conference meeting, he realized that someone is stealing from the company. Emotionally, this angers Donald, as evidenced by the Seven of Swords. Spiritually, the Hermit card confirms that he is trying to discover who is stealing from the company.

For the bottom row, which represents the technician's position, we see:

> Temperance
> The Chariot
> Seven of Pentacles

Ron considers himself a patient (Temperance), productive (the Chariot) and hardworking employee (Seven of Pentacles). There is no evidence in these cards that he has stolen anything. Quite the opposite, it shows him to be loyal to the company.

For the second row, Donald draws:

> Seven of Wands
> Page/Knave of Swords

The Veil/Truth Reading
Donald's Employee Issue

In positions 7 and 8, we find the Seven of Wands and the Page/Knave of Swords. These are assertive and expressive cards. Since this row addresses the idea that Ron's actions are making Donald suspicious, let us look a bit closer. The Seven of Wands could indicate that Ron does not get along with his coworkers and often tries to defend or justify his actions when confronted. The Page/Knave of Swords could indicate someone who talks or gossips too much. Although these are both negative qualities in an employee, the cards do not target any dishonest behavior. Emotionally, Ron may come across as unsociable and a bit reactive. Spiritually, for reasons not yet revealed, these cards suggest that he may not be a team player and tends to separate himself from his coworkers.

For row four, these cards were drawn:

Nine of Wands
Ten of Cups

In positions 9 and 10, the cards reveal information about Ron of which Donald is unaware, or has no control over. If there is a major problem brewing, it will often show up in these cards. Here we see the Nine of Wands and the Ten of Cups. Emotionally, these cards identify Ron's personal life as happy. Spiritually, these cards speak to Ron's devotion to the company, his strong work ethics (Nine of Wands) and his perception that, at work, he always does his best. There appear to be no underlying reasons to suggest that he is compelled to steal from the company.

In the middle row, these two cards were drawn:

The Fool
Four of Cups

In positions 11 and 12, we discover the truth. The Fool is sending a message to Donald that he should look elsewhere for the responsible party, since there is no indication whatsoever that Ron is stealing from him. The Fool card often suggests a new journey or, in this case, a new search. The Four of Cups card lays to Ron's right, and confirms that Donald is looking in the wrong direction. In this example, the person illustrated in the card is focused on the three cups before him rather than the obvious cup to his left. This represents Donald, who needs to take the focus off Ron and look around. Once he does, it will not be difficult for Donald to spot the actual thief.

Emotionally, this reading enables Donald to let go of a singular idea and his suspicions about Ron. Driven by the need to know who is stealing from him, he may be experiencing tunnel vision and needs to expand his search.

Spiritually, the cards remind Donald that, if he will look beyond his assumptions and review the facts, he will be protected from accusing the wrong person. The cards also infer that he will find the actual culprit if he allows Spirit to reveal his or her identity (Four of Cups).

Note that in this layout, had Ron been stealing from the company, more pentacles and swords would have appeared. As a rule, when a majority of cards in one suit or element appear, they typically reflect the nature of the question asked.

CROSSROADS READING

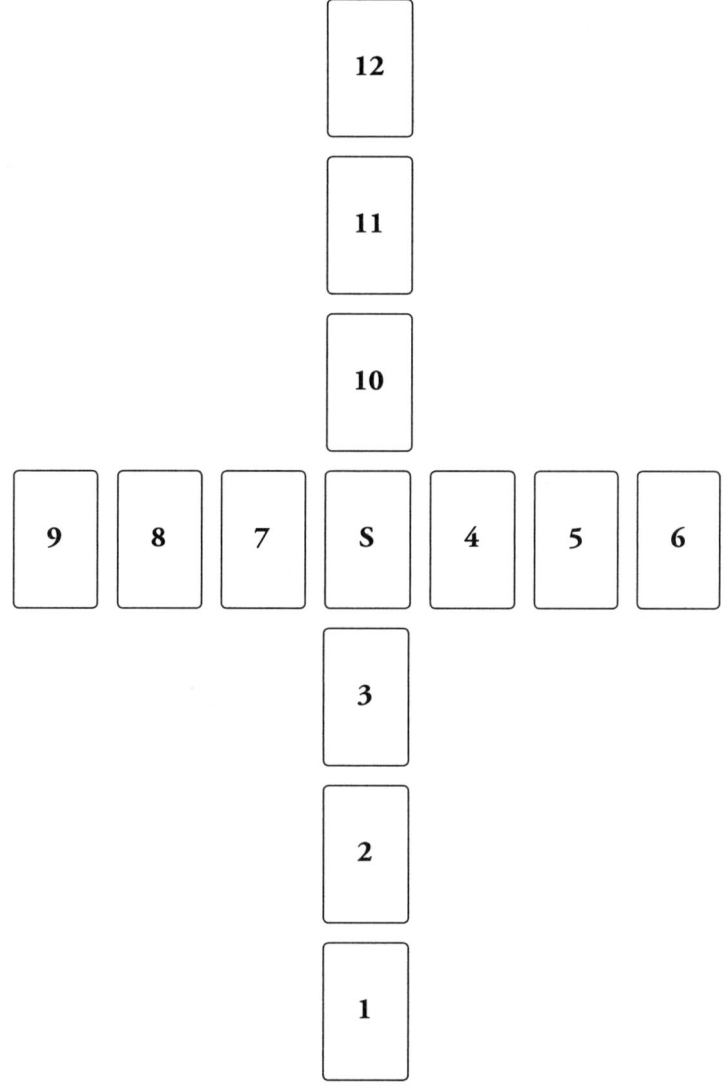

At some point, everyone finds themselves at a critical juncture in which the future may seem overwhelming or uncertain. The Crossroads reading enables one to focus on the possibilities, and outlines what one can expect from each path they are invited to take. The Crossroads reading can help point you or your querent in the right direction and offer insight into the challenges and advantages of each option.

Directions: Choose a significator that represents you or your querent's situation (See significator tables in appendix B) and place it in the center of the layout.

Shuffle the remainder of the cards and lay them out as illustrated, to form a cross with four arms, or pathways.

The southern path, cards 1, 2, and 3, represent the road you took to arrive at your current situation. (Note that the first row in the layout is read from bottom to top, while the remaining three rows are read from the center outward.)

The eastern path, cards 4, 5, and 6, represent the choice you or your querent is most drawn to, with card 6 representing the most probable outcome of this option.

The western path, cards 7, 8, and 9, signify the least desirable option, with card 9 representing the most probable outcome of this choice.

The northern path, cards 10, 11, and 12, outline a third choice for consideration, or reveal a new option for the querent. Card 12 will represent the most probable outcome if this direction is taken.

(Concept/Design: Louise Gilbertson)

Brooke's College Options Reading

Brooke is preparing to go to college next year, but cannot decide which school to attend. She has been accepted by one out-of-state university. She could also attend her local college while living at home, a less expensive alternative. Because Brooke is focused on higher education, she selected the World, (which represents this subject) as the significator for this reading.

After placing the World card in the center, she shuffled and then drew the following cards for the southern path:

Six of Swords
Eight of Wands
Knight of Cups

The southern row in the layout is read from bottom to top, while the remaining three rows will be read from the center outward. Cards 1, 2, and 3 speak to the reason Brooke finds herself at this crossroad. The Six of Swords indicates that she is nearing the end of her elementary education and wants to pursue a college degree once she completes high school. Swords represent intellectual aspects of life, so this card affirms that Brooke is preparing to move to a higher level of learning. The Eight of Wands in this reading is not so much a timing card as it is a reminder that time is running out, and that, the sooner she makes a decision, the sooner she can focus on preparing for college. The Knight of Cups signifies that her applications have been accepted and that she has been invited to attend both of the universities she is considering.

Emotionally, these cards indicate that her goals are within sight, and she needs to make the best decision possible. Spiritually, she wants to be ready when the Universe moves her to the next level of her development.

For the eastern path, Brooke drew these cards:

Ace of Swords
The Moon
Three of Swords

Crossroads Reading
Brooke's College Options

In positions 4, 5, and 6, the eastern path, we explore Brooke's first option, the out-of-state university. The Ace of Swords affirms that this school is her first choice. The Moon indicates that she knows little about this school and should do more research. The Three of Swords suggests that this school may be an unwise choice for her. Brooke wants to focus on a degree in animation, but, with two of these cards in the suit of Swords, this college is most likely geared toward intellectual, academic studies and less focused in liberal arts or creative degrees. Emotionally, these cards suggest that this particular school might be a disappointment if she expects to learn about animation. Spiritually, these cards are warning her not to move too quickly, as there is illusion surrounding her expectations about this university.

For the next row, Brooke drew these cards:

Eight of Pentacles
The Hermit
Four of Pentacles

Along the western path, cards 7, 8, and 9, we are looking at Brooke's least desirable option. She is somewhat reluctant to attend college locally, as she is ready to spread her wings. The Eight of Pentacles indicates that, not only would this option save money, it would provide a well-rounded education and the instruction she is looking for. However, the Hermit implies that this option would isolate her from campus life. If she lives at home while going to school, she may save money, but will not be on her own. The Four of Pentacles indicates that this school, though educationally sound, would block her from the full experience she is seeking.

Emotionally, these cards indicate that Brooke's growth would be limited if she chooses this option. Spiritually, the Universe is asking her to look beyond financial obstacles and seek out an option that will help her blossom in her chosen career and fulfill her longing for independence.

For cards 10, 11, and 12, Brooke drew:

Knight of Wands
Ten of Pentacles
Strength

The northern path of this reading suggests that there is a better option for Brooke. Note that the Knight of Wands and Strength cards both contain images of a lion. The lion represents strength, power, and stealth. The Knight of Wands is encouraging her to explore more options. The Ten of Pentacles indicates that in tandem with this third option a scholarship may be available. Because this card represents the idea of financial stability and security, this school may also offer grants or financial aid, eliminating her need to attend her local university based on cost. With Strength in the final position of this path, the most empowering school for Brooke has yet to be discovered.

This reading reveals that neither of Brooke's choices is ideal, and that she should explore more options. Emotionally, both of the established schools will be disappointing on one level or another (Three of Swords and Five of Swords). Spiritually, the cards are asking her to open herself up to a greater possibility, and ask the Universe to guide her to a school that will fulfill all her needs, educationally as well as personally.

Jane's Pregnancy Reading

Jane wants a baby, and her biological clock is ticking. Still single at thirty-six, Jane is considering artificial insemination. She has a high-powered and demanding career as a copy editor, so she wonders if adoption might be a better alternative. Of course, the old-fashioned way of conceiving a child would be Jane's preference, but, at this point, she sees no indication of that happening.

Jane selected the Empress, who represents motherhood, as her significator and drew the following cards for the southern path, cards 1, 2, and 3:

> Eight of Pentacles
> Nine of Pentacles
> The Hermit

The southern row of this reading outlines the path that has led Jane to this crossroad. She has spent her life focused on perfecting her career (Eight of Pentacles) and building her fortune (Nine of Pentacles). Now that Jane has reached success in both those areas, she finds herself alone and longing to share her world with someone. She has always wanted a child, so the Hermit illustrates her willingness to seek an alternative option to bring this dream to life. At this point, she is considering the biological aspects of having a baby, but the Hermit in this row suggests that she seek spiritual direction before proceeding.

For the next row, Jane chose these cards:

> Page/Knave of Wands
> Knight of Wands
> Three of Cups

Jane's idea to become artificially inseminated is addressed in the eastern row of this reading, comprised of the Page/Knave of Wands, the Knight of Wands and the Three of Cups in positions 4, 5, and 6. The Page/Knave of Wands suggests that this is an inspired option, while the knight of the same suit promises that, if Jane attempts to become pregnant through artificial means, she could be successful on her first try. The Three of Cups represents a positive outcome, as well as the possibility

Crossroads Reading
Jane's Pregnancy

that this pregnancy could result in multiple births, either twins or triplets (based on the three women in the final card).

Emotionally, these cards speak to Jane's strong desire to become pregnant by any means possible. Spiritually, they suggest that, if Jane decides to follow this path, she would be successful.

Jane then drew the following cards for the next row:

The Moon
Six of Swords
Nine of Swords

An alternate choice would be adoption. The western row of the layout suggests that this might be difficult, if not impossible, to accomplish. The Moon in position 7 warns that Jane may have misconceptions about the adoption process. The Six of Swords in position 8 defines this journey as long and arduous, with many obstacles. This card could indicate that, because she is single, it may be even harder for Jane to adopt. In position 9 we have the Nine of Swords, which suggests that she may be blocked every step of the way, and in the end, give up.

Emotionally, these cards represent a path that would most likely result in disappointment and frustration. Spiritually, they warn that this option is filled with illusion, misconception, and blocks she will not be able to move past.

For the final path, these cards were drawn:

The Fool
The Magician
The Emperor

The northern path of this reading alerts Jane to a third option for her to consider. Here we find three major arcana cards in positions 10, 11, and 12, which reveal this path as the most powerful. The Fool suggests that there may still be time for Jane to form a relationship, and that the Universe could shortly surprise her with a partner (the Magician) who also longs to be a parent (the Emperor).

This reading reveals that there are two options for Jane to consider more seriously, and one she will want to avoid. These cards advise her to keep in-vitro fertilization as a viable backup while she tries, one more time, to find a partner who shares her desire to be a parent. Emotionally, Jane is prepared to have this baby alone if necessary, but spiritually, the cards are asking her to consider the idea that a relationship could still come into the picture. Even if Jane starts the artificial insemination process and becomes pregnant, it will not diminish the possibility that a relationship may be in her future.

Elsie's Inheritance Reading

Elsie has just received a sizable inheritance from her uncle, and has many options to consider. Her first thought is to place it in a solid investment, but she does not feel that current economic conditions make any investment strategies "safe." She wonders if she should leave her job, take early retirement, and live off the inheritance. She is open to a third option, but has no idea what it might be. Elsie chose the Ace of Pentacles for her significator, a card that represents new money and new opportunities.

Then she drew these cards for the southern path:

> Death
> King of Swords
> Queen of Pentacles

The southern path of this reading, cards 1, 2, and 3 cards are Death, the King of Swords, and the Queen of Pentacles. This tells us what happened to bring Elsie to this crossroad. The death of her uncle (King of Swords) has left her a wealthy woman, represented by the Queen of Pentacles. Note that whether or not Elsie is an earth sign woman, the Queen in this reading indicates a woman of means.

For positions 4, 5, and 6, Elsie drew:

> Seven of Cups
> The Wheel of Fortune
> Five of Pentacles

The eastern path of this reading addresses the option of investing her inheritance money. The Seven of Cups suggests that Elsie may be overwhelmed as she tries to find the best investments. She may also be tempted to go on a shopping spree, which would leave little to invest. The Wheel of Fortune illustrates the concept that what goes up must come down, and that, at present, there is little stability in the stock market. The Five of Pentacles indicates that if Elsie invests the money, she could end up losing everything. Following this option would definitely not work for her.

Emotionally, these cards indicate that Elsie may not handle money well and that risking it in investments would put her back in the situation she is currently in, a

Crossroads Reading
Elsie's Inheritance

grave disappointment to her. Spiritually, the cards are warning her away from this option, indicating that her attempts to manage her funds could leave her in ruins due to karmic circumstances out of her control.

For the next option, these cards were drawn:

Six of Wands
The Devil
Nine of Pentacles

The eastern path would involve Elsie holding on to the money and taking an early retirement. The Six of Wands in position 7 indicates that she could have a battle on her hands if she follows this path. Whether Elsie ends up fighting herself, public opinion, or guilt for spending her good fortune, she could encounter difficulty making this transition. The Devil in position 8 suggests that if she makes this choice, she might become afraid or insecure about the future or start to second-guess herself. It also implies that people with less than honest intentions could steal money from her, or become friends with her based on her financial status. Elsie could lose a good portion of her inheritance if the wrong person came along and engaged her emotionally to spend the money. The Nine of Pentacles in position 9 represents abundance, but could also be a warning that if left to her own devices, Elsie may become indulgent or lazy if she takes this path.

Spiritually, the cards warn that Elsie and her money could soon part ways if she ignores her true purpose in life and takes the easy way out.

For the final row, these cards appeared:

Two of Pentacles
Eight of Pentacles
Knight of Wands

The northern path contains the Two of Pentacles, Eight of Pentacles, and Knight of Wands in positions 10, 11, and 12. As the line that represents a new option to consider, the first card, the Two of Pentacles, suggests that Elsie find a balance between the two paths she is considering. (The image in the card portrays a man weighing his options carefully.) The Eight of Pentacles suggests she continue to work, but that she may want to use some of the money to go back to school or open a business of her own. The Knight of Wands implies that she can still invest a portion of the money, but that spiritually, she should ask the Universe to reveal the best options for assured growth.

This reading will help Elsie formulate a more balanced plan for her future. We are not always forced to choose one path over another, even if it appears so when the time comes to make a decision. Emotionally, she can build the most security by using the money to expand her career options, taking additional training or starting a business of her own. Spiritually, Elsie will be investing in herself when she uses the money as a means to open her own business or advance her education, allowing the funds to open the door to a new life.

Three

ADVANCED READINGS

THE GYPSY'S MIRROR READING

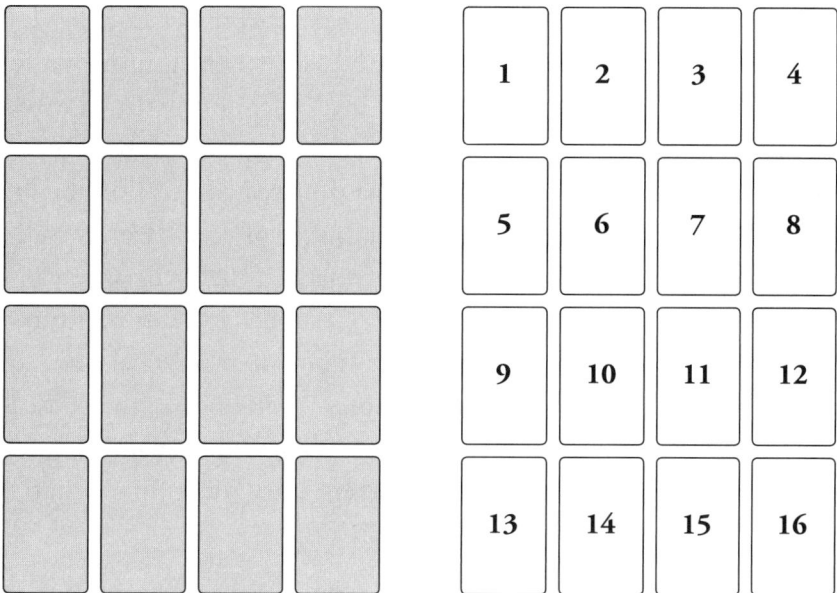

The Gypsy's Mirror reading is ideal for general readings and, because of its design, can address multiple aspects of a situation. On the left, sixteen cards are selected to represent the mirror in a face-down position. As the querent randomly picks from these cards and lays them face up on the right side as shown, they create the reflective and predictive Gypsy Mirror that can advise and direct them. This layout is especially effective with a querent who is willing to let go of physical control and rely on intuition to select cards.

Directions: Have the querent shuffle the cards while they concentrate on their question. If they want a general reading, have them ask Spirit to guide them in choosing the order of the cards to generate the best insight possible. From the top of the pile, have them lay out the first sixteen cards to form four rows of four cards each, face down on the left side of the table.

Ask the querent to select the cards one at a time, in random order, and place them face up in the numbered positions on the right side of the table. There are many ways to select the cards, but one of the most effective is to have the querent relax and move their hand slowly over the cards, using their intuitive skills to select the appropriate card. Another method would involve choosing the cards visually, as the querent's eye catches whichever card stands out as the one to be selected next.

Once all the cards have been turned over and placed in position, begin reading the horizontal rows first, taking note of the meaning of each card, as well as its relationship to surrounding cards. Each row represents a theme or aspect of the querent's question. If the querent has no specific questions, you can perform a general reading about some aspect of their spiritual, emotional, or physical lives.

If desired, you can also scan the cards for connections within the vertical and diagonal rows, again taking note of how the cards align and interact with each other. Once the reading is complete, suggest the querent learn more by meditating on the messages contained in this reflective Gypsy Mirror.

Brandon's General Forecast Reading

Brandon would like a general reading. He has no specific questions, but is looking for an overview of his life as it stands now, as well as what he can expect in the near future.

(When reading for a querent who offers no specific inquiry, invite them to be interactive in the reading. Do not hesitate to ask them to verify what you pick up, or to clarify cards that might have two or more meanings. As you work together, you will be able to offer your querent greater guidance, and in a faster and more complete way. I often encourage my querents to think of me as a doctor and tell me where it "hurts." This way, I can get down to the business of enlightening them.)

Brandon shuffled the cards, laid them out face down, and picked them in the following order:

King of Swords
Five of Wands
Ten of Pentacles
The World
Knight of Wands
Six of Wands
Knight of Pentacles
King of Pentacles
The Lovers
Strength
Justice
Queen of Swords
Eight of Wands
The Tower
Ten of Swords
The Sun

The first row contains the King of Swords, Five of Wands, Ten of Pentacles, and the World. Brandon is an Aquarius, so he is represented by the King of Swords. This card can also indicate that the first thing on Brandon's mind (swords) are struggles

The Gypsy's Mirror Reading
Brandon's General Forecast

(Five of Wands) of a financial nature (Ten of Pentacles). He is focused on retaining his financial standing in these economically difficult times (the World). This row indicates that he should be able to maintain his financial balance, as the cards do not predict any surprises in this area.

Emotionally, Brandon is aware of the economic state of the world and wants to protect his assets. Though he has not experienced any loss, he is intent on maintaining his security. Spiritually, these cards indicate a man with a strong standing in the physical world who is intuitively aware of the need to practice caution.

Row two consists of the Knight of Wands, the Six of Wands, the Knight of Pentacles and the King of Pentacles. Because these cards suggest energy (wands) and physical well-being (pentacles), this line addresses Brandon's health. The Knight and Six of Wands suggest that he is active, strong (note the image of the lion on the Knight of Wands card), and has a strong constitution (Six of Wands). The Knight of Pentacles implies that to strengthen his body (King of Pentacles), Brandon should increase his physical activity. He confirms that he has been eating better and working out, and the cards confirm his efforts are paying off.

Emotionally, the cards in this row represent someone who is paying attention to how his energy and well-being are enhanced by his movements and dedication to overall balance. Spiritually, the wands in this row represent a person who is in tune with all aspects of himself, and understands that his body is a temple which, when attended to, can house a stronger spirit and confidence as he moves through his days.

In row three we find the Lovers, Strength, Justice, and the Queen of Swords. Brandon is single and not currently dating, so we interpret these cards to be a message about his love life. Because three of the cards in this row are major arcana, there could be a karmic change in his status (the Lovers). He has been focused on strengthening himself and his financial position (Strength), and is now ready to begin an authentic long-term partnership (Justice).

Emotionally, these cards are encouraging him to invest more energy toward finding his true match (Queen of Swords). Though he does fine on his own, a partner would increase his emotional well-being. Spiritually, the three major arcana cards emphasize that this is an important area to work on, as it appears to be the only aspect of his life that has yet to come into being.

The last row of cards contains a warning of sorts, suggested by the Eight of Wands, the Tower, the Ten of Swords, and the Sun. Though these cards do not identify the source of this upset, the Eight of Wands implies that it will arise within a short time, perhaps two days, two weeks, or two months. The Tower and Ten of Swords speak to an abrupt and disappointing event, but the Sun assures Brandon he will experience a victory in this challenge. At this point in the reading, we could have drawn additional cards for more information about where this "storm" will hit, but Brandon decided he would rather not know more about it. I assured him he would know what it was when it happened, and to keep his focus on the positive affirming energy of the Sun.

Emotionally, these cards affirm Brandon's ability to bounce back when faced with unfortunate circumstances. They imply a positive attitude and inner strength. Spiritually, the cards forewarn him to be prepared for a sudden turn of events, and assure him, through the Sun and Eight of Wands cards, that he will be able to move through it with grace and protection.

This reading demonstrates how each row of the Gypsy's Mirror layout can address a different aspect of one's life, revealing specific messages and affirmations of progress. To discover more, we can view the cards as they fall in vertical rows.

Reading from top to bottom, the first column consists of the King of Swords, the Knight of Wands, the Lovers and the Eight of Wands. Here we see that if Brandon will invest his emotional energy into finding a relationship, he could experience success very quickly, anywhere from two days to two months. Spiritually, reading the cards in this vertical row affirms once again, that it is time for him to expand his life in this area.

Column two consists of the Five of Wands, the Six of Wands, Strength, and the Tower. Again we see a warning to Brandon that there is a challenge he will soon have to face. With the Strength and Tower cards located here, these major arcana cards affirm that spiritually, he can handle whatever comes along.

In column three of the layout, we find the Ten of Pentacles, Knight of Pentacles, Justice, and Ten of Swords. Because the first two cards are pentacles, this row addresses finances or health. The Ten of Swords can often indicate surgery, so I asked Brandon if he was facing a potential surgery or had any health concerns. He mentioned that he was looking into outpatient surgery to correct a torn ligament in his knee, as it has been limiting his movement. He had been putting it off until he could afford the cost of the surgery, as represented by the Ten of Pentacles. The Knight of Pentacles addresses movement, while the Justice card refers to balance, and promotes the idea that this surgery would indeed correct the problem. Based on this line, the cards are encouraging him to address this issue in the near future.

Emotionally, Brandon is agreeable to having the knee surgery, but the Ten of Pentacles and Justice cards confirm he wants to have the money available before he proceeds. Spiritually, the cards are supporting this, pointing out that though the surgery is not an immediate necessity, having it done will restore mobility to his knee.

In the final column, the World, King of Pentacles, Queen of Swords, and the Sun paint an overall picture of a happy future. The World refers to Brandon's life as a whole, and the balanced effort he is putting into each area. The King of Pentacles speaks to a stable and prosperous financial future, along with continued and improving physical health. The Queen of Swords represents the new love that could be entering his life soon, and the emotional and spiritual joy it will bring (the Sun).

Carolyn's Fidelity Reading

Carolyn is happily married with a fulfilling career. At a marketing seminar recently, she encountered Pete. The chemistry between them was electric. They have been assigned to work together on a project that brings them into weekly contact. There has been a bit of flirtation between them, but Carolyn has no intention of becoming involved with Pete. However, she now finds that she cannot stop thinking or fantasizing about him. She would like to know why this attraction is so strong, how to keep things in perspective, and if there is a way she can break free of the mental obsession it is creating.

After shuffling and laying the first set of cards face down on the table, she drew cards in the following order:

Five of Cups
Two of Pentacles
Queen of Wands
Three of Wands
Ten of Wands
The High Priestess
Seven of Pentacles
Knight of Wands
Five of Pentacles
The Lovers
The Sun
Eight of Swords
The Chariot
Queen of Pentacles
Ten of Swords
The Devil

In row one we find the Five of Cups, Two of Pentacles, Queen of Wands, and Three of Wands. This situation has created quite a bit of emotional confusion for Carolyn (Five of Cups), and although she is attempting to maintain her balance (Two

The Gypsy's Mirror Reading
Carolyn's Fidelity

of Pentacles), her passions are running wild (Queen of Wands). Though Carolyn is not acting on her feelings (Three of Wands), this row identifies her turmoil. Spiritually, the wands in this row suggest she's engaged in a struggle between her desires and her morals, and finds herself watching and waiting for some type of intuitive direction (Three of Wands).

The cards in row two are the Ten of Wands, the High Priestess, Seven of Pentacles, and Knight of Wands. The burdens of Carolyn's passion (Ten of Wands) will need to be dealt with on a spiritual level (the High Priestess). Because she will be working with Pete on a regular basis (Seven of Pentacles), Carolyn must find a way to channel her attraction in a way that will not create trouble. Pete appears in this row as the Knight of Wands, an intense person she views as sensually overpowering and thus, potentially dangerous.

The third row consists of the Five of Pentacles, the Lovers, the Sun, and the Eight of Swords. Here we see that Carolyn is highly aware of the pain and sorrow

(Five of Pentacles) she would create emotionally, were she and Pete to become lovers (the Lovers). The Sun implies that there is a higher spiritual purpose to this situation but because Carolyn is attempting to process her feelings intellectually, she may not be able to see it (Eight of Swords).

The final row is comprised of the Chariot, Queen of Pentacles, Ten of Swords, and the Devil. The Chariot suggests that Carolyn is being pulled in two directions, while the Queen of Pentacles asks her to set new boundaries around this situation. Once she does, the mental obsession will dissipate (Ten of Swords), and the emotional fear (the Devil) surrounding Carolyn's feelings for Pete will subside. The Devil card also serves as a warning, asking her to consider things from a spiritual angle, to avoid a situation that could cut her off from her inner truths.

This reading outlines all aspects of the situation (spiritual, mental, and physical), and offers direct advice: she must set up stronger boundaries. Clearly, Carolyn will have to take responsibility for whatever unfolds, and must keep her priorities (her marriage and integrity) in sight. If she can learn to abstain from fantasy and keep her focus on Spirit, these current difficulties will begin to fade.

Now let's take a look at this reading from a different angle, reading the cards in their vertical rows to gain further insight.

From top to bottom, the first column then becomes the Five of Cups, Ten of Wands, Five of Pentacles, and the Chariot. As defined by the cards, these are challenging messages that foretell sorrow, burdens, loss and being pulled in two opposing directions, describing the very situation Carolyn is facing.

Column two contains the Two of Pentacles, the High Priestess, the Lovers, and the Queen of Pentacles. These cards imply that she will be able to maintain her balance, as long as she uses spiritual methods to do so. Her emotional desire to take Pete as a lover will eventually fade because Carolyn is grounded in her values, priorities, and commitments.

In column three we see the Queen of Wands, the Seven of Pentacles, the Sun, and the Ten of Swords. This line suggests that it is all right for Carolyn to appreciate, work, and interact with Pete. In the event this relationship moves into dangerous territory, she is spiritually capable of ending it.

The final column in this interpretation contains the Three of Wands, the Knight of Wands, the Eight of Swords, and the Devil. This line reminds Carolyn to step back and look at the other side of this equation. She is focused on her own feelings, but needs to take a closer look at where Pete is coming from. He is definitely enamored of her, and could be caught up in his own fantasies. With the Devil appearing as the final card, Pete is certainly in a position to do her emotional harm if she allows it. These cards do not indicate that he is a bad person, but they do suggest that he is looking out for himself and his own best interests. Carolyn should do the same.

In this layout, there are no cards present to indicate any past life karma or a connection of souls, such as the Six of Cups or the Wheel of Fortune (see card combination tables in appendix C). If enough cards appeared to suggest this type of karmic connection, one might want to explore the relationship further with the Past Life reading in the advanced reading section.

Because we see no higher purpose or spiritual past-life connection between Carolyn and Pete, we can assume that this situation is designed exclusively for Carolyn's emotional and spiritual growth.

Melinda's Divorce Reading

After nine years of marriage, Melinda and her husband Adam are considering divorce. They are currently in counseling, and Melinda would like to know if there is a chance they will reconcile, or if they will decide to proceed with the divorce.

After shuffling the cards and laying them out, she selected these cards in the following order:

Nine of Pentacles
King of Pentacles
The Empress
Ten of Swords
Seven of Swords
Five of Swords
Knight of Pentacles
Ace of Cups
Eight of Pentacles
Queen of Pentacles
The Hierophant
Seven of Wands
Judgement
Four of Swords
Two of Pentacles
Six of Cups

Row one contains the Nine of Pentacles, the King of Pentacles, the Empress, and the Ten of Swords. Interestingly enough, the couple has been married for nine years, as depicted by the Nine of Pentacles. Adam is a Capricorn, so the King of Pentacles signifies him, while the Empress represents Melinda. The Ten of Swords verifies that they are talking about ending the marriage. Spiritually and emotionally, these cards represent the difficult situation Melinda and Adam find themselves in.

In row two we find the Seven of Swords, the Five of Swords, the Knight of Pentacles, and the Ace of Cups. The Seven of Swords represents deception or thievery,

The Gypsy's Mirror Reading
Melinda's Divorce

while the Five of Swords is usually associated with divorce or separation. These two cards indicate that Melinda and Adam will move ahead with their decision. The Knight of Pentacles, a relocation card, suggests that soon, one or both of them will move to a different residence. The Ace of Cups is normally thought of as the start of a new love. In this reading, it could indicate the newfound emotional stability Melinda carries. It asks her to focus on loving herself and putting her own needs first, instead of hanging on to a relationship which has run its course.

In the next row, we have the Eight of Pentacles, Queen of Pentacles, the Hierophant, and the Seven of Wands. These cards indicate that to receive the money she deserves out of the divorce settlement (Eight of Pentacles), Melinda (the Queen of Pentacles), will have to enlist a skilled lawyer (the Hierophant) to protect and defend her rights (Seven of Wands). These cards are sending an intuitive message from Spirit, reminding her to make sure she takes action to get all she is entitled to.

In the final row, we find Judgement, the Four of Swords, Two of Pentacles, and Six of Cups. This indicates that once the divorce is final (Judgement) and Melinda has had a period of recovery (Four of Swords), balance will be restored to her life (Two of Pentacles) and suggests, through the Six of Cups, that a new and more loving relationship will soon come her way. Spiritually, the Judgement card is asking her to allow the Universe to transform her world during this difficult situation, and promises (Two of Pentacles and Six of Cups) that if she does, better things await her.

Though this reading does not give Melinda a way out of her situation, it does reveal the gifts that will come to her as she moves through this life-changing event, and promises a more fulfilling relationship in the future.

DREAM INTERPRETATION READING

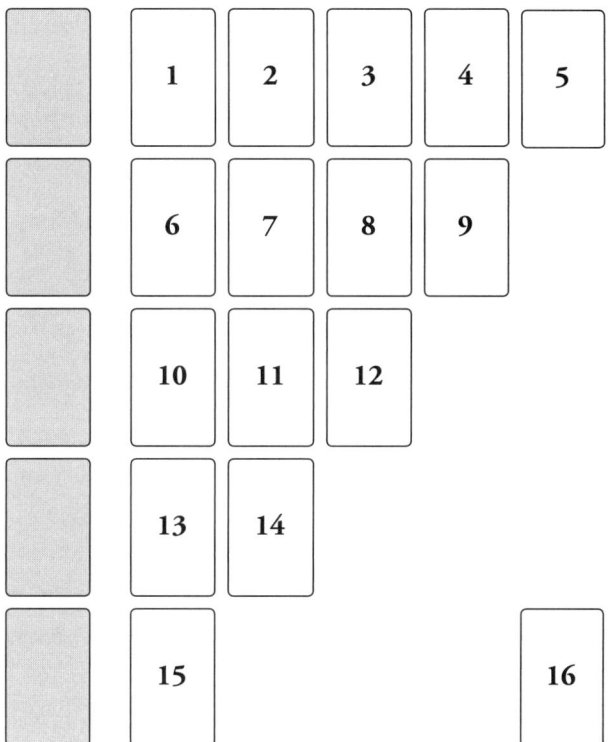

Although their messages are often steeped in symbolism, dreams carry important information and glimpses into our psyches. The Dream Interpretation reading is designed to provide a broader view of one's dreams, so the dreamer can move beyond the intellectual impressions they receive to gain greater understanding.

Directions: Shuffle the cards as you concentrate on the images and feelings of a particular dream you would like to know more about. Cut the deck into five piles, laying them out in a vertical pattern, one below the other, as indicated in the illustrations. Choose the top card from any pile and lay it in position 16 at the far right of the layout. This card will represent the overall theme of the dream.

Draw five cards from the first pile and lay them out horizontally across the table to form the first row. From pile two, draw four cards, from pile three, three cards, two cards from pile four, and one card from pile five, as shown in the illustrated examples.

Read the cards from left to right, with these guidelines in mind:

> Row One (Cards 1–5) identifies outside influences that may have triggered this dream, along with spiritual insights about the dream.
>
> Row Two (Cards 6–9) refers to intellectual insights contained in the dream.
>
> Row Three (Cards 10–12) outlines emotional insights of the dream.
>
> Row Four (Cards 13 and 14) addresses any fears or concerns the dream may have triggered.
>
> Row Five (Card 15) offers advice and reveals more messages contained in the dream.

After the reading is complete, review the card at the bottom right corner of the layout (card 16) for a final comment or affirmation as to the messages contained in the dream.

You may also want to review the cards vertically, in columns, for further information about the dream.

Audrey's Spiritual Journey Dream Interpretation

Audrey dreamt she was taken on an incredible spiritual journey, back through past lives and ancient times to the places where she initially learned the spiritual knowledge that is now beginning to emerge in her current life. She would like to learn as much as she can about this dream because she suspects that she was, in reality, astral projecting back through time.

Audrey shuffled the cards and divided them into five piles, setting a card to the right as the theme indicator.

For row one, she drew the following cards:

The High Priestess
Eight of Wands
King of Wands
Seven of Pentacles
Eight of Cups

The first card is the High Priestess, confirming Audrey's belief that this dream focused on her spiritual growth and psychic abilities. The Eight of Wands implies flight or rapid movement, reflecting her travel through different lifetimes. In her dream, there was a man who accompanied her on her journey, as represented by the King of Wands. The Seven of Pentacles acknowledges Audrey's spiritual efforts and predicts that she is about to reap great rewards for the seeds she has sown. The Eight of Cups in this row refers to the many gifts that have come from her previous efforts, and the spiritual fullness which now surrounds her.

In row two, we find:

Five of Pentacles
Four of Cups
Ace of Swords
Three of Pentacles

The cards in row two reveal the mental insights hidden in this dream. Intellectually, she is eager to move her spiritual practices to the next level. The Five of Pentacles

Dream Interpretation Reading
Audrey's Spiritual Journey

indicates that Audrey has been in a rut, going around in circles, frustrated by her inability to move forward. The Four of Cups tells us that this dream heralds a breakthrough for her. When she least expected it, Audrey was taken on a dream journey to a new dimension. The Ace of Swords encourages her to freely express her newfound wisdom and enlighten others as to what she has experienced. The Three of Pentacles foretells of a new beginning, an internship of sorts, that will move Audrey to the next level of her spiritual and intellectual development.

These cards appeared in row three:

Six of Cups
Two of Pentacles
Temperance

The cards in row three define the emotional insights of the dream. The Six of Cups indicates that on her dream journey, Audrey crossed paths with many souls from past lives who shared important information with her. The Two of Pentacles reveals her newfound ability to maintain balance as she travels between alternate planes of reality. Temperance reminds her that in order for her to move back and forth between these worlds, she will have to remain patient and balanced (also inferred by the Two of Pentacles).

Row four contained these two cards:

King of Swords
Seven of Wands

This row addresses Audrey's fears. Here, the King of Swords and Seven of Wands both represent a struggle of some type. She may be fighting with herself, torn between advancing metaphysically and maintaining what she has already learned. In her dream, she argued with a strong and powerful man (King of Swords), and recalls having to defend herself against him (Seven of Wands). Her fear is that if she moves forward with her spiritual development, she may encounter opposition or criticism.

In row five we have:

The Queen of Wands

Because Audrey is an Aries, we interpret this card as representing her. The advice this dream extends to her is that Audrey must be true to herself and honor her special gifts. This card verifies that her experience was more than a dream; it marked her passage into a higher level of spiritual awareness and ability.

The theme card was:

Nine of Wands

The Nine of Wands depicts someone who has, through years of experience, built a solid spiritual foundation. Audrey moves in alignment with the Universe, and now feels ready to share her spiritual truths. Reflecting her new level of awareness and power, this card predicts that Audrey is about to experience an amazing transformation into a new plane of existence, where she can enlighten and encourage others.

Jacob's Grandmother Dream Interpretation

Jacob recently lost his grandmother, with whom he was very close. A few months after she passed away, he dreamt she made a call to him on his cell phone. Jacob was very excited to hear her voice on the other end. He told her he was surprised she could call, and asked her how she was doing. His grandmother replied that she was doing well and that she often came to look in on him. Then, over the phone, she started to share a recipe with Jacob, something she had often done in real life. The ingredients and instructions became confusing as she used terms such as "one cup of kindness," "two tablespoons of patience," and "a dash of humor." He asked her if she could e-mail the recipe, a practice she frequently did when she was alive. She replied that she couldn't send an e-mail, so he would have to listen closely and remember the recipe. Then, suddenly, Jacob's grandmother told him she had to go, but would visit with him again soon. At this point he woke up. The dream was so intense that Jacob could feel the cell phone against his ear, but when he reached for it, it was not there.

Jacob would like to know if his grandmother truly visited him in the dream, or if his mind and emotions were playing tricks on him. Either way, he's searching for deeper meaning in this dream.

After shuffling, Jacob divided the deck into five piles and chose a theme card, laying it to the lower right side of the layout.

Then he pulled these five cards for row one:

> Five of Pentacles
> The Star
> Four of Cups
> The Chariot
> Death

The first row of cards identifies any outside influences that might have precluded this dream, along with spiritual insights contained in this vision. The day before his dream, Jacob found himself missing his grandmother (Five of Pentacles). His greatest wish (the Star) was that he could speak with her. The Four of Cups suggests

Dream Interpretation Reading
Jacob's Grandmother

that in Jacob's awakened state, he was unable to hear his grandmother but once he was asleep, she would be able to talk with him. The Chariot implies that his grandmother is now able to move back and forth between the spirit and earth planes, something she has learned to do since her passing (Death).

To explore the intellectual insights of the dream, Jacob drew these four cards for row two:

The Hermit
The Hanged Man
Queen of Wands
Ace of Wands

These cards address the question he asked about the dream, "Was this truly a message from my grandmother?" The Hermit represents someone who is seeking spiritual enlightenment and affirmation. The Hanged Man suggests that when Jacob was in a suspended state (dreaming), his grandmother's spirit (the Queen of Wands) did, indeed, come to him with an important message (Ace of Wands).

Row three contained:

Three of Swords
Nine of Wands
Two of Wands

Emotionally, the first card here refers to Jacob's pain over the loss of his grandmother. The Nine of Wands usually refers to a person with great spiritual depth and strength. However, in this case, we want to look a bit closer at the image to see how it ties specifically into Jacob's dream. This card depicts a structure comprised of many small pieces that when bound together, form a strong and protective fence. It may be that the "recipe" Jacob's grandmother shared with him was actually for living; the main ingredients being tenets of wisdom. With the Two of Wands in the last position (again, a sign of duality that represents the narrow line between heaven and earth), Jacob may be faced with important choices, and this "recipe" could aid him in making these decisions.

The cards in row four were:

Nine of Pentacles
The Moon

One of Jacob's greatest sorrows is that he will never again spend time with his grandmother. The Nine of Pentacles speaks to her ever-abundant and joyful spirit. Jacob has many wonderful memories of his grandmother, and his melancholy is a result of her absence. The Moon in this position implies his sadness is an illusion—there is nothing to fear, because his grandmother's spirit now possesses the power to contact him through his dreams (another trait of this particular card).

The card in row five was:

King of Wands

This is a card of breakthrough and empowerment and in this case, affirms Jacob's grandmother truly visited him through a dream. It appears she has reached a new level of spiritual ability and can now communicate with him from the other side.

The theme card was:

Judgement

The supernatural nature of this dream is confirmed in the final theme card, Judgement. This card refers to a breakthrough, a resurrection, and the passage between the spirit and earth planes. It also confirms that Jacob's grandmother did visit him, offering him important information that will serve him well in the future.

Barbara's House Dream Interpretation

Barbara has been dreaming about a particular house for years. Each time it happens, the house appears in a different form or condition, but she knows it is the same one. At times the house appears grand and majestic; other times, it is deserted, with broken windows and decaying boards. In her most recent dream, Barbara was walking through this house again, and noticed that this time, it had been divided into apartments. In one of the apartments, she found a secret staircase leading to a basement. Descending to the basement, she discovered that illegal aliens were running a business out of her home. She tried to get them out of the house, but there were too many, and a struggle ensued. After a time, she was able to rid her house of the intruders, but its structure was now in shambles. At this point, Barbara woke up.

She would like to know more about this recurring dream, particularly what kind of message the latest one is sending her. She shuffles the cards and lays them out as shown in the illustration.

These are the cards she drew for row one:

> Seven of Swords
> Six of Wands
> Queen of Cups
> Two of Cups
> Three of Swords

These cards address both the spiritual aspects of this dream, as well as any influences that might have activated it. The Seven of Swords represents the people operating an illegal business in her home who are, in essence, stealing from her. The Six of Wands depicts Barbara's successful battle to remove them from her house. The Two of Cups and Three of Swords do not reflect events in the dream, but serve as hints of what might be going on in Barbara's personal life. When questioned about these two cards, she mentioned that in the days preceding the dream, a man she had been dating for two months admitted he was seeing other people on the side. Barbara ended the relationship.

Dream Interpretation Reading
Barbara's House

Because Barbara dreams about this house on a regular basis, it is likely that it reflects where she is in her life at any given time. It could be that, at the time she dreamed of a majestic home, her life was in order and things were going well, but when she dreamed of the same house in ruins, her world was falling apart. The fact that she just broke up with someone could connect that event to this dream on a number of levels. In the dream, her home had been divided into apartments. Correspondingly, she could have been trying to compartmentalize herself in this relationship. A part of her feels betrayed by this man. While she was making plans for the future, he had a secret agenda (a secret staircase), and was, unbeknownst to her, dating other women (running a "business on the side" while engaging with her).

Keep in mind that when one dreams of a house, its levels reflect certain aspects of the person themselves. While the upper level of a home (attic, second, or third floor) represents spirituality, the basement can refer to things that are hidden away, either in the subconscious or when one is being deceived or deceiving themselves.

This row suggests that her dream is sending a spiritual message to her about the recent breakup in a form most recognizable to her, namely, the reoccurring house in her dreams.

In row two, the cards were:

Ace of Swords
Two of Swords
Knight of Swords
Eight of Pentacles

Row two addresses the dream's intellectual insights. The Ace of Swords, Two of Swords, and Knight of Swords indicate thoughts and ideas. The Ace of Swords reflects the awareness she received that she was being deceived (the Two of Swords), both in the dream and in real life. The Knight of Swords, a card that represents anger or aggression, reveals the purpose of this dream is to help her express what she has been holding in. Though she has to accept her boyfriend's position, she does not have to endure it. When she became aware of his actions, she chose to protect herself, but was not able to express her true feelings to him. As a result, her feelings were processed through this dream, where it was safe to vent her frustrations, and run the "intruders" out of her home. The Eight of Pentacles suggests it's time for Barbara to work on herself, and turn her back on a situation that is unacceptable to her.

For row three she drew:

The Magician
Nine of Cups
The Devil

Row three reflects the emotional insights in this dream. Here we find the Magician, the Nine of Cups, and the Devil. Emotionally, the man she hoped could provide a magical and abundant relationship turned out to be a disappointment. Barbara's dream reflects this experience, when she discovered a secret staircase leading to the basement of her house, and came face-to-face with a shocking discovery involving deception and dishonesty (the Devil).

These cards appeared in row four:

> Four of Cups
> Knight of Pentacles

The cards in this row address fears that have arisen from this dream. Here we have the Four of Cups and Knight of Pentacles. In the first card, the woman gazes sadly at the three cups in front of her. For Barbara, this reflects the disappointment and sorrow she feels about the loss of her relationship. Her fear is that she will never have a long-term partnership, even though this card indicates that another person is coming soon, depicted by the fourth cup emerging from the heavens above. Her second fear involves how to move forward after a personal disappointment. In Barbara's dream, she is distraught to find her basement invaded, but goes to battle. Even though she is outnumbered, she prevails in reclaiming her house. This reflects her ability to go back out into the world in search of true love, even though the odds appear to be against her.

The fifth row card was:

> Judgement

The Judgement card implies that this dream, and the breakup, are designed to create an important breakthrough for Barbara. After discovering strangers in her house, her drive to protect it speaks to how much she values the home. In the same vein, ending the relationship with her boyfriend speaks to how much she values herself.

The theme card was:

> The Fool

The Fool defines this dream as symbolic of a new journey on which she is about to embark. It sends a message that it's time to release the past and set out on a new path. In her dream, she reclaims her house, but realizes there's much to do to restore it. In real life, Barbara understands she must pick up the pieces, practice more self-love, and commit to starting over on her quest to find true love.

CHAKRA/HEALTH READING

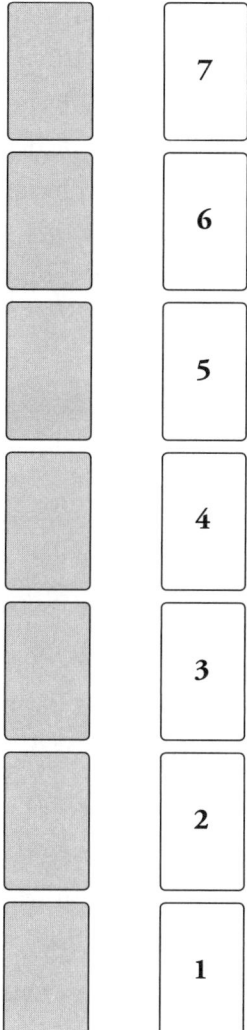

The Chakra/Heath reading is designed to evaluate the state of one's physical, emotional, and spiritual health through the seven chakras or energy centers of the body. This layout will also address each area of your body and alert you to any problems.

In this reading, the cards are read starting with the root chakra and moving upward to the crown chakra. This method allows the reader to systematically move through the querent's energy centers and identify any physical or emotional issues before addressing spiritual aspects of the situation. However, you may read the chakras in any order you prefer, as each card in the corresponding position is specific to that energy center.

The seven chakra energy centers vibrate to one of the seven colors found in a rainbow or prism. Each chakra is located in a specific part of the body and is responsible for maintaining those areas as defined here:

The Root Chakra/Red—"Life Force"—Physical aspects, the lower body (legs, feet), the groin, male and female genitalia, and the root or base of the spine

The Creation Chakra/Orange—"Desire"—Creative aspects, the pelvis, the reproductive glands, hips, and lower back

The Power Chakra/Yellow—"Power"—Spiritual source and empowerment aspects, the stomach and middle organs of the body, middle back

The Heart Chakra/Green—"Love"—Emotional aspects, the heart, breasts, lungs, and upper back

The Will Chakra/Light Blue—"Communication"—Will and expressive aspects, the neck, throat, mouth, and nose

The Intellectual Chakra/Indigo—"Conscious Thought"—Mental health aspects, thought, intellect, processing center, the brain, eyes, and forehead

The Crown Chakra/Purple—"Enlightenment"—Spiritual aspects, the third eye, connection to the Universe and one's developing soul (Note: This chakra is located just above the head and rules the spiritual aspect of one's life. Therefore, it is not connected to any physical part of the body.)

If you have trouble interpreting a card while performing this reading, you may pull additional cards from the corresponding pile for more information. For example, if the Devil appears in position six, the intellectual chakra, you may be entertaining fear or worry. Pulling an additional card such as the Hanged Man or Hierophant may indicate the need for more meditation or offer a directive that you turn your worries over to the Universe to eliminate these troublesome thoughts. You may pull as many cards from the corresponding deck as needed until the situation and its solution become clear.

When you encounter blocks, troubles, or stagnant energy in a certain chakra, you can use the color associated with it to heal or improve the situation. For example, if you discover blocks in your creative chakra, you can surround yourself with orange, its associated color. Eat more orange foods, add orange candles, pillows, or decorative items to your environment, or wear gemstones of this color, such as citrine stones or Mexican garnets to help restore this chakra.

Directions: Shuffle the cards as you concentrate on your overall health and balance. Cut the deck into seven piles, laying them vertically from one to seven. (To maximize your layout space, you can also lay them out horizontally.)

Pull one card from each pile for an overall view of your current state of balance. As an example, if the Sun appears in a position, your overall health and energy for that energy center is operating at its best.

Read each card as it corresponds to the chakra you are investigating. If needed, pull additional cards from the pile for more information.

Brenna's Chakra Reading

Sarah has recently noticed that her seven-year-old daughter Brenna is becoming short-tempered and impatient. She wonders if Brenna is going through a growth spurt or if she might have an underlying physical ailment contributing to her moodiness. Sarah shuffles the cards as she concentrates on her daughter, then cuts the deck into seven piles.

These are the cards she drew:

7. Crown chakra—Queen of Swords
6. Intellect chakra—Eight of Wands
5. Will chakra—The Sun
4. Heart chakra—Knight of Wands
3. Power chakra—The Devil
2. Creation chakra—Eight of Pentacles
1. Root chakra—Strength

Beginning with the root chakra, which defines physical health, we see the Strength card. This indicates that Brenna's overall health is fine, and that there are no problems lurking beneath the surface. With this factor eliminated, we can look further for the true cause of her recent moodiness.

The Eight of Pentacles in position 2 indicates that Brenna's creation chakra is also working well. This card represents someone who is busy mastering their skills, and affirms the idea that she may be experiencing a growth spurt or moving through a natural stage of her development. Based on this card, I would suggest to Sarah that when Brenna is angry or frustrated, her mother encourage her to draw a picture about her feelings. Since Brenna loves to draw, this could be a creative way for her to express and process her emotions.

The Devil lies in position 3 and points out the initial area of conflict. Because the Devil represents fear or a sense of being undermined and, based on the fact that it is located in her power chakra, Brenna may be experiencing a shift of consciousness as she becomes more aware of the world around her. As a toddler, she may not have thought much about anything but her own immediate needs, but now that she is in school, she is encountering situations outside of her experience.

Chakra/Health Reading
Brenna's Chakra Reading

At this point, I counsel Sarah to ask Brenna how things are going at school, whether she is getting along with her playmates, and if any of the children are bullying or threatening her. Because anger is often the outcropping of fear, getting to the source of her uneasiness could improve the situation rather quickly. I recommend to Sarah that she encourage Brenna to eat more yellow food, or to purchase a necklace or bracelet with a yellow stone that Brenna can wear at all times. This will add an extra layer of protection around Brenna, and make her feel less fearful or vulnerable.

The Knight of Wands occupies the position of the heart chakra. This card affirms that, in her heart, Brenna is lively, optimistic, and creative. The Knight of Wands represents a happy home life, and a feeling of safety and protection that supports her emotional balance. Knights are often considered assertive or aggressive, which affirms the idea that, when Brenna feels afraid, she reacts in anger or frustration.

The Sun card resides in Brenna's will chakra position, which can help Sarah get to the heart of her daughter's frustration. This card implies that Brenna can express herself openly, and that, if someone asks her, she will be happy to tell them what is going on. However, because she is so young, she may not be able to determine why she reacts to certain things. This chakra vibrates to light blue, so I suggest to Sarah that dressing Brenna in this color will empower her daughter to identify and express her concerns more quickly.

The intellectual chakra position is occupied by the Eight of Wands. This card indicates a growth spurt that Brenna is experiencing. New information is coming in at lightning speed, making it difficult for her to process and sort through her emotions and reactions. As she tries to keep up with schoolwork, developing friendships, and the changes going on in her body, her perceptions may be affected by an overstimulated mind.

To balance out the mental gymnastics Brenna is experiencing, I suggest Sarah establish a transition time for her daughter. When Brenna gets home from school, Sarah can create a special place or activity to quiet her down. Whether it involves milk, cookies, and conversation, or a five-minute "cuddle with her favorite teddy bear" session, a break can offer Brenna a chance to catch her breath before her day continues.

With the Queen of Swords in the spiritual chakra position, (Sarah's significator card, as she is an Aquarius), Brenna relies on her mother for guidance. She trusts her mother and knows that she can come to Sarah with her problems. The challenge for Brenna lies in being able to recognize and identify what the trouble is. Sarah is in a unique position to teach Brenna alternate ways to express and process her anger, by providing her with tools and guidance for situations that are outside the realm of Brenna's experience.

Overall, fear seems to be at the core of this problem, so if Sarah and Brenna can locate the source of her fear and eliminate it, Brenna's bouts of anger should soon fade away.

David's Back Problem Reading

David is recovering from a recent operation on his lower back. The procedure went well, but instead of feeling better, he feels worse. He is concerned that the operation did not resolve his painful back issues and may have exacerbated the problem instead. Although this reading is directed at a major health problem, we may discover other areas that are contributing to his difficulties. David concentrates on his back pain while he shuffles the cards and then cuts the deck into seven piles.

These are the cards he drew:

7. Crown chakra—Justice
6. Intellect chakra—Two of Wands
5. Will chakra—The Hanged Man
4. Heart chakra—The Fool
3. Power chakra—Eight of Wands
2. Creation chakra—The Tower
1. Root chakra—Five of Pentacles

The root chakra defines David's physical health, and the Five of Pentacles in this position confirms his current issue. Note that in this particular deck, the Five of Pentacles is emanating a light, and in effect, targeting the area of his recent surgery. It also suggests that there is still pain in that area, so we know that David's complaints are valid. As an initial suggestion, I recommend that his diet include more red foods (the color that rules this region) or that he wear red clothing to hasten the healing process.

The Tower occupies position two, depicting the state of David's creation chakra. This indicates that physically, his lower body has endured a shock, but defined by the transformational message of the Tower, this surgery has been a necessary part of the healing process. Emotionally, his frustration has made him doubt the success of this surgery. Because his movement continues to be limited, his creativity is blocked, and his ability to heal may be challenged. I advise David to increase his intake of orange food or to add vitamin C, a known healing agent, to his daily supplements.

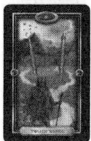

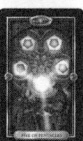

Chakra/Health Reading
David's Back Problem

We find the Eight of Wands in the power chakra position. This indicates that David has not given his body enough time to heal. He may be impatient after having suffered with this ailment for so long. This card indicates that a two-week or two-month period of healing will yield the desired outcome. I remind him that he is in a healing process and must be patient, and that he should see improvement within the next few months.

David's heart chakra is represented by the Fool. Emotionally, he is anxious for a fresh start. There are many activities he has had to refrain from because of his back problems, and we know he is anxious to return to a full and active life. He was hoping to come out of the recovery room and go straight to the tennis courts, but will have to be patient for a while longer. At this point we discover a repeating theme in this reading, having to do with his fear that the problem remains. Because he has suffered for so long, and wants it resolved, his perception of the situation is compromised.

This idea is repeated in David's will chakra, indicated by the Hanged Man. He remains in limbo—not the outcome he expected. Although all the cards indicate he is healing, he fears the worst, because it has not yet happened. He does not feel that the doctors are sympathetic to his complaints, and believes he is not being heard. There are no blocks indicated in this area, so I encourage him to practice a healing mantra. This area rules expression and voice, so I directed him to say out loud, three or more times a day, "I am healthy, strong, and able to move without pain." Expressing this belief will trigger the same confidence to infiltrate in his intellectual chakra, where it can then begin to affect and improve other areas of the body.

The Two of Wands sits in the intellectual chakra position. David has a choice when it comes to what he chooses to believe is happening. He can decide that the surgery was not successful and that he is destined to a life of pain or, he can choose to trust that the problem has been resolved and that, within a few months, he will improve. (Note that we focus on the Eight of Wands and the Two of Wands as indicators of when he should experience a healing. The Eight of Wands is normally a timing card, and the Two of Wands appears to confirm this number, as they are of the same suit and numerological value. Always look for confirmation in the cards, based on their numbers, suits, images, and positions in the reading.)

At this point, I encourage David to perform a guided meditation each day and to visualize restored movement and optimum health. I suggest that he imagine himself on the tennis court, going for walks, and moving without pain. If he does this twice a day for five or ten minutes, he will witness faster progress in his recovery.

Spiritually, he knows that this problem will be resolved, affirmed by the card in the crown chakra position, Justice. The image on this card features a female embodiment of justice, with light and energy flowing from her hands out to a targeted area, interpreted in this reading as David's lower back. (This could refer to any part of the body, as its basic message is that spiritual healing is taking place, and that the outcome will be what he is hoping for.) Justice in this position suggests that, in combination with the surgery he has just had, David should engage in more spiritual methods to speed up his healing.

This reading reveals that somewhere deep within, David knows he is healing, but is still waiting for evidence of progress. If he embraces more spiritual practices to improve his attitude and outlook about the situation, he can get out of his own way, bypass his unfounded fears, and heal in the fastest and most effective manner possible.

When you perform the Chakra/Health reading, pay close attention to the location of each card, and the area it is addressing. If there were still physical troubles that David needed to investigate or, if the surgery had not been successful, this would have been indicated in the root or creative chakra card.

Anne's Depression Reading

Anne's overall health is good, but recently she has experienced bouts of depression that seem to appear without warning. With the Chakra/Health reading, we should be able to determine where these emotions are originating, and how to alleviate them.

After shuffling and dividing the deck into seven piles, Anne turns over the following cards:

7. Crown chakra—Four of Wands
6. Intellect chakra—Seven of Cups
5. Will chakra—Knight of Wands
4. Heart chakra—Strength
3. Power chakra—Five of Pentacles
2. Creation chakra—Nine of Pentacles
1. Root chakra—Ten of Swords

One additional card was drawn from pile one, the root chakra, for clarification:

Seven of Pentacles

Beginning with the root chakra, we find the Ten of Swords. This card indicates trouble in the area of her physical body. Anne may not be getting enough exercise, or she could be experiencing pains or aches in her lower body. The Ten of Swords alerts us to a physical problem that could be manifesting itself in other areas. Emotionally, she could be processing the pain into feeling paralyzed, hopeless, or frustrated, which could be contributing to her bouts of depression. Spiritually, this card indicates a feeling of defeat, at the most basic of levels.

For more specific information, we drew a second card from the first pile, the Seven of Pentacles, which confirms that this is a physical problem, and reveals that she is out of balance. Anne either needs more exercise or, on the other hand, could be doing too much physical labor, which is draining this energy center. At this point, I advise Anne that to address this area she integrate more of the color red into her diet, wardrobe, and surroundings.

Chakra/Health Reading
Anne's Depression

For the creation chakra, Anne drew the Nine of Pentacles. This card suggests that the energy in this area is working well. Intellectually, she recognizes the abundance that surrounds her, but emotionally she cannot understand where these episodes of depression are coming from. Spiritually, she is in a creative cycle, able to envision something and bring it to life.

The Five of Pentacles appears in the power chakra position. This represents a lack of connection with her power source, Spirit. Anne admits that lately, she finds herself unmotivated, has difficulty feeling empowered, and cannot seem to make the personal changes she longs for in her life. Physically, she would like to engage in more exercise and lose a few pounds, but emotionally she gives up her commitments fairly easily. This is the second area where depression could be manifesting itself, especially if her attempts to empower herself always seem to fail. In this case, I suggest Anne add more yellow to her surroundings, to see if it will counteract some of the blocks she struggles with. I also suggest that she increase her meditation practices, asking the Universe to help her take action on her personal goals.

In the heart chakra position, we find the Strength card. This is the only major arcana card in this reading, and implies that emotionally and physically, her heart is in excellent shape. She is in a supportive relationship that contributes to her emotional well-being, and at this point, could be the most stabilizing aspect of her life. When other areas in life feel stagnant or difficult, she can turn to her partner for comfort and validation.

The Knight of Wands occupies the will chakra position. This card suggests that Anne possesses a talent and passion for the art of expression. As a motivational speaker, she has no trouble sharing her insights with others. The Knight of Wands in this position affirms that through her sharing, she has the power to uplift and inspire others. Spiritually, this card suggests that Anne honor her psychic gifts by acting on her intuitions.

Looking at the intellectual chakra position, we find the Seven of Cups. This may indicate a third area where depression could be forming. The Seven of Cups suggests that she has a lot on her mind, and that she tends to worry about things she has no power to control. This can create a sense of helplessness, which could then undermine her confidence and eventually turn into self-pity or blame. To accelerate healing in this area, I advise Anne to add indigo to her environment as a form of color therapy, and to practice the art of turning over whatever she cannot resolve or change to the Universe. The intellect chakra responds well to mental processing, so I encourage her to keep a daily journal to track these patterns of depression, which will make it easier to see what is triggering them.

Anne's crown chakra is represented by the Four of Wands, which speaks to a strong spiritual foundation. The Universe is guiding her movements, she is protected, and she has everything she needs. Though she may feel at times that Spirit does not hear her (based on the Five of Pentacles in her power chakra position), her belief and trust in the Universe remains strong.

This reading reveals which areas are functioning properly (her creative, heart, will, and crown chakras), and identifies where some adjustments are called for (her root, power, and intellectual chakras). Armed with this information, she can now focus on healing the troubled areas targeted in this reading. With color therapy, additional meditation or journaling, along with a willingness to let go of things she has no control over, Anne should start to experience relief from her bouts of depression and soon, witness a return to emotional balance.

PAST LIFE READING

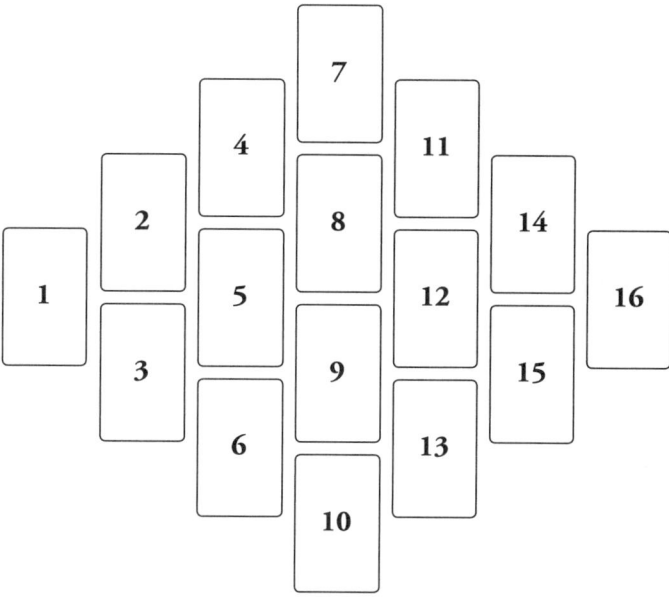

The Past Life reading is designed to explore incarnations from previous lives. Our souls carry the knowledge and experiences we collect throughout our many lifetimes. Investigating them through the Past Life reading can help you to understand why certain people are in your life, the reason you are drawn to a certain place or historical era, or the origination of unexplained fears or patterns. Whether you would like to know if you have spent past lives with your partner, why you are afraid of heights, or the reason you gravitate toward anything connected with ancient Greece, for example, this reading can offer more insight.

During this reading, you will have to rely on your intuition to connect the dots. As the images of the tarot cards unlock memories from your subconscious and reveal past connections, new information will emerge. To get the most information from this past life reading, you'll need to trust your instincts and pay close attention to the images on each card.

Look for patterns or traits from the past that also appear in your current life. For instance, if the reading reveals that you traveled across the American prairie during the nineteenth century in search of a better life, you may also have left a hometown in your present life to seek greener pastures. If you find that you have unexplained phobias (fear of heights, claustrophobia, etc.) or chronic health problems, these could also be rooted in the past. For example, if you suffer from obesity or anorexia currently, these could be manifestations of having starved to death in a past life. Likewise, a hesitation to swim in deep waters could come from having drowned in an earlier incarnation.

Perhaps you wonder whether your parents were with you in a past life. If so, their significator cards should appear in the reading. Depending on what cards fall next to the significator, you may discover that, in a past life, your mother was your sister, or your father was your son. Take note of any court cards (king, queen, knight, and page/knave) or major arcana personality cards (the Magician, High Priestess, Empress, Emperor, and Hierophant) that appear in the reading, as they will identify people currently in your life, who were also present in the past life you are researching.

As you move through the cards in this reading, you will need to play the detective. Look for repeating colors or numbers in the cards that offer more clues. Use your imagination to fill in the blanks, based on whatever images, scenes, or dialogue come into your consciousness.

After completing a past life reading, you should notice a shift in your emotions as well as your awareness over the next few days; often, more memories will come back to you. This is an affirmation that you did indeed experience the past life you researched during this reading.

Directions: Shuffle the cards as you concentrate on a person, location, or event from a past life that you would like to know more about. Pull sixteen cards from the top, and lay them out as shown in the illustrations.

Cards 1, 2, and 3 offer information and clues to help identify the specific past life you are tuning in to.

Cards 4, 5, and 6 should identify an important event that took place in this past lifetime. More often than not, this event has repeated itself in your current life, validating a connection between the present and the past.

Cards 7, 8, 9, and 10 will identify people you know or situations that appear familiar to you, confirming that you have experienced them in a past life.

Cards 11, 12, and 13 will contain more information regarding your question, or continue to reveal how certain events from this past life are replaying themselves in the present.

Cards 14, 15, and 16 will reveal why your querent feels a strong connection to a certain person or place, or why your querent suffers unfounded fears or perceptions in the present.

Michael's WWII Past Life Reading

Michael has had a fascination with World War Two since he was a young boy. His best friend Andrew shares his passion for this period in history. Michael would like to know if they both lived through this historic event and if they were best friends in that past life as well.

Michael focused on his friend Andrew while he shuffled the cards, as well as the fascination he carries for the historic war.

For rows one and two, he drew these cards:

Two of Pentacles
Six of Swords
Six of Wands

To confirm that Michael has tuned in to the WWII past life, we examine the cards in positions 1, 2, and 3. The first card is the Two of Pentacles. Since it is a two, it can stand as the idea of a world war. The card in this deck depicts a snake wrapping around and separating two pentacles. Although the basic definition of this card is balance, it can also refer to someone who is weighing a decision. The snake might represent Adolf Hitler, known for surrounding, invading, and capturing other countries. The two pentacles could represent opposing sides or warring factions. Upon examining cards 2 and 3, we find additional clues to indicate that we have located Michael's past life during WWII.

The Six of Swords could represent a journey over water, and the Six of Wands indicates a person heading into battle. The fact that WWII lasted six years, from 1939 to 1945, is confirmed by the appearance of the two number six cards. Michael must have traveled across water (Six of Swords) to reach this battle (Six of Wands). Because this suggests that he was fighting for the Allied forces, it is likely that his past life originated in either the United States or the United Kingdom.

For row three, these cards were drawn:

Eight of Cups
The Sun
Queen of Swords

Past Life Reading
Michael's WWII Past Life

In cards 4, 5, and 6 we examine the important lessons Michael experienced in this past life, as well as significant people from both his past and his present lives. Card 4, the Eight of Cups, reflects Michael's adventurous spirit. He felt confident in his decision to leave his home behind to fight in this world conflict. Interestingly, in his current life, he also left his homeland and relocated to another country, evidence that this pattern repeated itself.

The Sun suggests a victory. Note the man with a sword in one hand, a flag in the other, and a crown on his head. This portrays someone who was victorious in all he did, and who exhibited a competitive spirit. In this lifetime, Michael is also successful, and often jokes about his competitive side. Having been on the victorious side of the conflict during this past life, this could be the source of his confident demeanor in the present.

Card 6 is the Queen of Swords. This represents someone he knew in this past life, who can also indicate a person that is in his life now. Upon investigation, Michael identified this card as his girlfriend, who is a Gemini. There are no cards in the reading to explain what role she played in his life during WWII. Note, however, that both she and the man in the Sun card hold their swords up victoriously, indicating a match or connection of some type. Most of their interaction could have been by mail (swords indicate communication) or by wire, so it is possible that, in this past life, she was the sweetheart he left behind when he went off to war, one who supported and encouraged him through the letters they exchanged. (Of course, in this lifetime, the two have graduated to e-mail!)

For row four, these cards were drawn:

- Three of Pentacles
- King of Cups
- Two of Swords
- Knight of Wands

Cards 7, 8, 9, and 10 identify people or situations relating to Michael's question about his friend Andrew. Here we find the Three of Pentacles, The King of Cups, the Two of Swords, and the Knight of Wands. Because this row contains the card that represents Andrew, indicated by the King of Cups (Andrew is a Scorpio), we can surmise that these two men were friends in this past life.

These cards suggest that Michael met Andrew during some kind of internship, depicted by the Three of Pentacles. They probably met during basic training, or were in the same outfit or camp during the war. The King of Cups tells us that Andrew reached out to Michael first, and that they became fast friends. The Two of Swords might indicate that they lost touch during a battle and, for a time, Michael didn't know where Andrew was. That scenario was repeated in this lifetime, when he and Andrew lost touch during their college years. Michael went to school while Andrew enlisted in the air force, repeating the course his life took in the WWII past life we are investigating.

The Knight of Wands implies an enduring friendship, both in spirit and heart, and suggests that Michael and Andrew have traveled through many lifetimes together as close and supportive friends. This card also implies they have fought many battles together and that when one or the other encounters conflicts in present life, they are there for each other.

The following cards appeared in row five:

> Strength
> Five of Pentacles
> Four of Swords

Cards 11, 12, and 13 tell us more about what happened between Michael and Andrew during this past life. The Strength card indicates that they both went off to war in good health, ready to defend their country. The image on the Five of Pentacles suggests difficult trials, severe weather, and feelings of sadness over the devastation they witnessed while at war. It could be that these harsh conditions compromised either Michael or Andrew's health. This is indicated by the Four of Swords, which represents a time of rest and healing after a challenging event. Note the man sitting under the tree, his battle flag draped over it, indicating that these cards address postwar times. Though Michael enjoys good health in this lifetime, his friend Andrew does not, so this row could be referring to health problems Andrew suffered after the war, which are now repeating themselves in his current lifetime.

These cards were drawn for rows six and seven:

> Five of Swords
> Judgement
> The Fool

The final three cards in this layout (14, 15, and 16) complete the story of Michael and Andrew's past-life friendship during WWII. (Note that because Michael asked only about this world war, the cards are just outlining this particular time period.) The Five of Swords indicates that when the war ended, it was a bittersweet victory. Judgement was passed and Michael returned home to begin a new phase of his life (the Fool). Michael can relate these cards to experiences in his present life in which he has battled issues with health, finance, or family. Each time, he was victorious. Once he overcame a certain strife, a new cycle of life began for him. Because

Andrew does not appear in the final three cards, it may be that when the war ended, he and Michael went their separate ways, only to meet up again fifty years later in this lifetime.

Allie's "Lost" Past Life Reading

Allie has a problem: she gets lost all the time. Even when she is armed with specific directions, the first time she attempts to visit a new location, Allie finds herself driving in circles. When this happens, she is overcome by panic, which adds to her confusion, making it even harder to find the address. Allie wonders if past life research can identify a karmic reason for this phenomenon and hopefully, bring it to an end. While she shuffles, Allie concentrates on the sensation of panic she experiences when she gets lost.

For rows one and two, she drew:

Ten of Cups
Knight of Pentacles
King of Pentacles

Cards 1, 2, and 3 identify the past life where this problem first appeared. Notice that the Ten of Cups, Knight, and King of Pentacles are predominately green. In the Ten of Cups, we see a rainbow of gold chalices, as well as gold shields in cards 2 and 3. This calls to mind the "pot of gold at the end of the rainbow." Based on these clues, we can surmise this to be a past life Allie spent in Ireland.

In this past life, Allie was surrounded by love and abundance, living a simple life in the countryside. The king may represent her father, while the knight might be a brother. If we glance at the rest of the cards in the reading, we spot a card that confirms she had a sibling (the Six of Cups in position 13), displaying a boy and girl playing in the grass. There is a general sense of safety and protection. Allie has no siblings in her current lifetime, but does have a friend who feels like a brother to her. At some point, she may want to investigate whether she and this friend shared this or another past life together.

In row three we find:

Three of Pentacles
Four of Swords
The Empress

Past Life Reading
Allie's "Lost" Past Life

Cards 4, 5, and 6 refer an important event that took place in this past life. The Three of Pentacles could indicate an age (pentacles representing the physical aspects of life), while the Four of Swords suggests an illness. In this past life, Allie may have become very ill around the age of three. The Empress in position 6 depicts a motherly figure. The look on the Empress' face suggests concern, care, and nurturing. When Allie became sick, her mother nursed her back to health. Allie recalls a number of times when she was sick in her current life, and how her mother nursed her back to health, including an episode with scarlet fever when she was two or three. Remember, cards in this row address an identifying event that has usually repeated itself in this lifetime.

Row four contained these cards:

The Emperor
The Tower

Ten of Wands
The Fool

The Emperor, the Tower, Ten of Wands, and the Fool (cards 7, 8, 9, and 10) make up the center row. Three of these four cards are major arcana, suggesting a major shift in Allie's world during this past life. From what we can see, her father (the Emperor) ran into some trouble. Based on the appearance of the Ten of Wands (burdens) and the Fool, her father may have lost everything and, at some point, the family had to start over. Though these cards do not reveal the nature of the trouble, clearly it was serious enough for them to pull up stakes and move (Ten of Wands) in search of greener pastures. Allie mentions that, during her present life, when she was around the age of six, her father moved the family across the country, in search of a better job.

These cards appeared in row five:

Four of Cups
Four of Wands
Six of Cups

In positions 11, 12, and 13 we have the Four of Cups, the Four of Wands, and the Six of Cups. This row of cards addresses the event that corresponds with her question, "Why am I always getting lost and, why do I panic when it happens?" The Four of Cups can represent boredom, as well as an unexpected gift from the heavens. Because the person in this image is at rest and, based on the fact that it is followed by the Four of Wands, we can conclude that her parents found a place to live and were making a start for the foundation of a new home. Literally or figuratively, as the family began putting up the structure, Allie may have found herself bored and gone in search of something to occupy her time. The image in the Six of Cups suggests she joined forces with her brother and went off to play.

Rows six and seven contained these cards:

Two of Swords
Five of Wands
Death

The final three cards (14, 15, and 16) reveal what happened next, as well as the root cause of Allie's problem. The Two of Swords implies that while she and her brother were playing, at some point, Allie looked up and found herself alone. Unsure of which path would lead her home, she realized she was lost. The Two of Swords illustrates her indecision and suggests that, once darkness fell, she was unable to find her way home (indicated by the blindfolded person shown in this card). After trying unsuccessfully to find her way home, (the Five of Wands) the cards suggest that she gave up and perished in the woods (Death).

Armed with this new information, it is easy to see why Allie panics when she gets lost. This past life memory, still ingrained in her subconscious, tells her that if she gets lost, she will die. It may be that in order to correct this problem, Allie will need to rely on landmarks or stores for direction, rather than street names or numbers.

Soon after this reading, I spoke with Allie to see how things were going. She told me that she still gets lost on a regular basis but, thanks to the information she received in this past life reading, she no longer panics when it happens.

Corey and Jeff's Past Life Conflicts Reading

Although Corey and Jeff are brothers, they have never gotten along. Their mother attributes it to sibling rivalry but Jeff feels it runs deeper than that. No matter what attempts he makes to get along with his older brother, Corey is not interested. Because of this, family gatherings are strained. Jeff would like to know if remnants of a past life are contributing to this situation, as he cannot find a reason for their distance in this current life. He feels that if he can discover the root cause, peace will be restored to the family. Jeff focused on his and Corey's childhood together as he shuffled the cards for this reading.

For rows one and two he drew:

Seven of Wands
Empress
Page/Knave of Swords

Card 1 is the Seven of Wands. This card contains the image of an older man, representing Corey, the elder brother. He is defending himself and appears to be in conflict, confirming that we are looking at the past lifetime in which the feuding between Corey and Jeff began. The card in the number 2 position is the Empress, while the Page/Knave of Swords occupies position 3. The Page/Knave of Swords depicts a younger man, in this case, Jeff. It appears that the trouble between Jeff and Corey also involved their mother (the Empress).

One gets the impression that in the past life we are researching, Corey and Jeff's mother may have been a young girl whose attention the brothers were competing for. At her feet, we see a heart engraved with the astrological symbol of Venus, suggesting that she may have been a love interest that came between the two brothers.

Considering the clothing of the characters, and the house depicted in the background of card 3, this deck appears to have an eighteenth-century feel to it, suggesting that this lifetime took place somewhere in the 1700s in Europe or colonial America.

Past Life Reading
Corey and Jeff's Past Life Conflicts

In row three, we have:

Three of Cups
Knight of Pentacles
The Lovers

The Three of Cups, the Knight of Pentacles, and the Lovers (cards 4, 5, and 6) reveal a time when Jeff, Corey, and his mother were friends, rather than family members. However, at some point, there was a change (Knight of Pentacles) and both Corey and Jeff fell in love with the mother (of course, in this lifetime she was a peer, not a parent). At this point in the reading it seems that in this past life as well as in the present, Corey and Jeff have often found themselves competing for their mother's attention.

Row four was comprised of:

The Star
King of Pentacles
Seven of Pentacles
Two of Cups

The Star, King of Pentacles, Seven of Pentacles, and Two of Cups (cards 7, 8, 9, and 10) again identify the two brothers, as well as the events that preceded their original quarrel. While Corey (represented by the King of Pentacles) daydreamed about making this girl his bride, Jeff worked to amass his fortune (Seven of Pentacles). Once he had made enough money, Jeff boldly approached the girl that both brothers adored, and proposed marriage to her (Two of Cups). Because the King of Pentacles is depicted gazing upwards, while the Seven of Pentacles contains an image of a man looking directly into the future, there is a possibility that, while Corey entertained visions of someday approaching this girl, Jeff took direct action and was first to ask this girl to be his bride.

These cards appeared in row five:

Page/Knave of Cups
Six of Swords
Two of Swords

The Page/Knave of Cups, Six of Swords, and Two of Swords (cards 11, 12, and 13) describe what happened next. Unaware of the engagement between this girl and his brother, Corey approached her with a proposal of marriage. He was met with resistance (Six of Swords), which left him feeling devastated and confused (Two of Swords). As it turns out, in their current life, during high school, there were a few instances when Jeff unknowingly took girlfriends away from Corey, unaware that his brother was interested in them as well.

Rows six and seven held these cards:

The Devil
Knight of Swords
Seven of Swords

The end result, depicted by the Devil, Knight of Swords, and Seven of Swords (cards 14, 15, and 16) indicates the hatred (Devil) and rage (Knight of Swords) Corey felt when he discovered what he felt was a deception on Jeff's part (Seven of Swords). From these cards we can imagine that Corey swore never to forgive Jeff, which subconsciously continues to affect their relationship. When Corey was displaced by Jeff's birth in their current life, it shifted much of his mother's attention away from him, and the pattern established in the past life began to repeat itself. This would explain why Jeff has always sensed resentment coming from Corey.

Now that Jeff has a better idea of where these negative feelings originated, he may be able to smooth things over with Corey by stepping back and allowing his brother and mother to interact more frequently. Though the knowledge of what happened in this past life may not resolve the problem, Jeff no longer blames himself for their inability to get along.

CHANNELING CHALICE READING

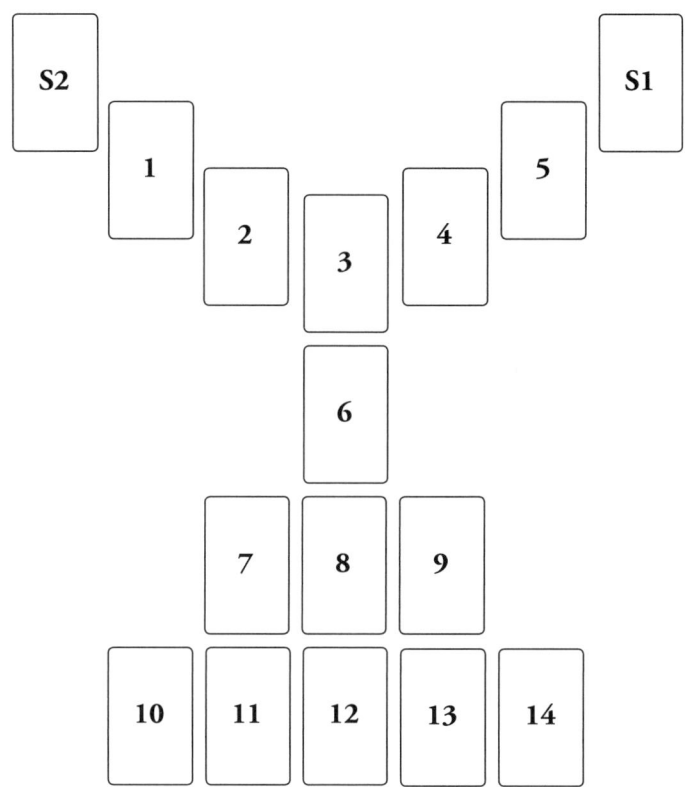

The Channeling Chalice reading is designed to open a channel between you and the spirit world, allowing you access to loved ones who have crossed over, personal spirit guides, or higher levels of your own spiritual self.

If you are using this reading to contact a loved one, it is sometimes helpful to have a possession of theirs nearby. If you do not have one, playing music or lighting incense of a scent that was special to them can add to the layout's effectiveness.

Trust your instincts as you read, and be open to receiving the messages or images that come during the reading. These signals validate that you have made contact with this special person and can trigger specific memories that you or your querent shared with them.

Directions: Begin by selecting a significator (see significator tables in appendix B) to represent the person who has crossed over. If you are reaching out to your spirit guides or your higher self, place the High Priestess or the Hierophant in the significator position to the right. Place the significator that represents you or your querent to the left.

Cards 1–5, the "cup" of the chalice, confirm that the querent has made a connection. In some manner, these cards should reflect the identity of the spirit being sought.

Cards 6–9, the "stem" of the chalice, will offer a personal message from the spirit to you or your querent.

Cards 10–14, the "base" of the chalice, contains important information for you or your querent, reveals the future, or answers questions you ask of this spirit.

The Channeling Chalice reading is designed to open a gateway to the other side. Once you have completed the reading, you or your querent will be able to continue a mental dialogue with the spirit guide or loved one who has been contacted.

Len's Channeling Session with his Father, Harry

Len lost his father, Harry, in a car accident. Because Harry's death was sudden, Len was left with many unanswered questions. Also, as the oldest son in the family, Len finds himself embroiled in conflicts with his mother and siblings over Harry's estate. He would like to honor his father's requests in these matters but, because Harry had no will, Len is unsure of what they are.

Len and Harry are both Aquarians. Because they are represented by the same significator, Len chooses the King of Swords for his father and the Knight of Swords for himself. Len has a pocket watch of his father's, and places that on the table before the reading. He concentrates on Harry, shuffles, and draws the cards.

In the cup of the chalice (Cards 1–5), we will receive confirmation that contact has been made. Here we find:

Harry, Significator 1—King of Swords
Len, Significator 2—Knight of Swords
The Fool
The Wheel of Fortune
The Chariot
Seven of Swords
Death

In the cup of this reading we see that Len has made a connection with his father. These cards lay out the scenario of Harry's car accident and, because four of the five cards are major arcana, the extreme circumstances that surrounded his death. The Fool suggests that Harry left the house that day, unaware of the profound karma that lay ahead (Wheel of Fortune). While driving to work (the Chariot), someone ran a red light and Harry's life was stolen (Seven of Swords). The Death card not only depicts the result of the accident, it confirms that Len is speaking with his father from the spirit world.

Channeling Chalice Reading
Len's Channeling Session with His Father Harry

In the stem of the chalice (cards 6–9) we have:

Ten of Cups
Three of Wands
Three of Cups
Six of Pentacles

The first thing Harry would like Len to do is send his love to the family (Ten of Cups). He acknowledges that Len is now responsible for dividing the assets and is in need of guidance (Three of Wands). The Three of Cups identifies Len's three sisters (note the three women dancing in the card) and their hopes of receiving large inheritances. Harry advises Len to be generous with the money (Six of Pentacles). This card also suggests that Harry is content with the way Len is handling his affairs.

In the base of the chalice (cards 10–14), we will discover the answers Len is seeking from his father. Here we find:

Nine of Pentacles
Four of Wands
Six of Wands
Five of Cups
Ace of Cups

The first card in this section depicts a woman standing in a field of pentacles. This suggests that Len give the bulk of the estate to his mother and that he make sure she is taken care of.

The image on the Four of Wands suggests a home in the country. Len mentions a cabin his family owns that his father promised he would inherit. This card suggests that Harry wants the cabin to go to Len. Harry is warning Len in card 12, the Six of Wands, that there will most likely be battles over these decisions; he asks Len to be strong. Because this card falls next to the Five of Cups, it can also be read as a request from his father that Len fight the sadness he is feeling as a result of Harry's death. He knows there will be periods of grief, but Harry is asking Len not to dwell in sorrow.

In the final card, the Ace of Cups, Harry again sends his love and reminds Len that he is not gone, but merely existing in a different dimension now. The ace represents new beginnings, and, in this position, it is Harry's way of affirming that their love for each other will never die. Rather, their relationship will transform itself into a new type of spiritual connection, one that is beyond either of their experiences.

Caden's Channeling Session with His Aunt Susan

Caden misses his Aunt Susan. When Caden was eight, his eighty-year-old aunt passed away peacefully in her sleep. Caden recalls their walks through the apple orchard behind her house and the bedtime stories Aunt Susan read to him. Recently, Caden has been looking for a special pen she gave him when he was a boy, but it seems to have disappeared. He wants to channel his Aunt Susan to see how she is doing, let her know he is about to start college, and ask her if she knows where the pen might be. He selects the Queen of Cups for his Aunt Susan, born in July, and the Knight of Pentacles for himself. He shuffles the cards and lays them out.

In the cup of the chalice (Cards 1–5), we receive confirmation that Caden has made contact with his Aunt Susan. Here we find:

> Aunt Susan, significator 1—Queen of Cups
> Caden, significator 2—Knight of Pentacles
> Three of Pentacles
> Eight of Cups
> Nine of Swords
> Seven of Pentacles
> Four of Wands

As we review the cards in this section, our goal will be to match known connections between Caden and his aunt to the images on the cards. The Three of Pentacles speaks to an intern, someone who is in a learning process. We interpret this card as acknowledgment that Caden was a young boy when he and his aunt shared time together. The Eight of Cups could also indicate Caden's age, as well as Aunt Susan's age at the time of her passing, him being eight years old and her being eighty. In the image, we see a collection of cups behind him—some upright and some tipped over. These represent the emotional connection he and his aunt had for eight years. The boy in the card is turned away, looking out over an empty valley, as if he is waiting for someone or something to return. Caden recalls that his parents waited a few months to tell him Susan had passed away. During that time, he waited anxiously for his aunt, who never returned. This is an important confirmation, as it reveals his

Channeling Chalice Reading
Caden's Channeling Session with His Aunt Susan

Aunt Susan knew he sat and waited for her after her death, which no one else noticed except Caden.

Though it typically implies blocks, the Nine of Swords in this reading confirms that Aunt Susan used to read bedtime stories to Caden. Since swords represent all forms of communication, the multiple swords hanging over a person in bed refer to the many books she read to him, and confirms that she remembers this too. The Seven of Pentacles in this deck depicts a woman picking fruit from a tree, illustrating and affirming Caden's memory of their walks through the apple orchard. The Four of Wands speaks to a strong foundation. When Caden saw this card, he recalled that he and his aunt used to make "forts" in her backyard, with four posts and a sheet. He

ADVANCED READINGS | 227

had forgotten this, but we see it serves as another indicator that in this reading, he is talking directly with his Aunt Susan.

In the stem of the chalice (cards 6–9), we find a special message to Caden from his aunt. Here we have:

> Nine of Cups
> The Emperor
> Four of Cups
> The World

The Nine of Cups depicts a man making a toast, which can be interpreted as Aunt Susan applauding Caden's successes. Interestingly, the Nine of Cups also indicates the number of years that have passed since she died. He has grown into a fine young man (the Emperor) and she is very proud of him. She tells him to expect the unexpected (Four of Cups) as he prepares to head off to college (the World). This affirms that she has been watching over him, and knows he is preparing to embark on a new journey.

In the base of the chalice (cards 10–14) we discover the answers Caden is seeking from his aunt. These cards are:

> Page of Swords
> The Hermit
> The Chariot
> Temperance
> Seven of Cups

Because Caden asked about a special pen his Aunt Susan had given him, we assume that the Page of Swords represents this pen. The man in this card holds a sword, similar to a pen, pointing downward, in the suit of the tarot that represents communication. The Hermit depicts a man searching for something, which tells us that his aunt is addressing his question. The Chariot appears in the next position, suggesting that Caden look in his car. (In our follow-up session a few weeks later, Caden confirmed that he did indeed find the pen in the glove box of his car.)

The appearance of the Temperance card suggests that Susan is always looking after Caden, serving as his guardian angel.

The final card is Aunt Susan's way of sending her love to Caden, along with wishes for a bright future. While the Seven of Cups typically refers to feeling overwhelmed or facing multiple worries, in this reading we interpret it as an abundance of wishes and emotions. If we examine the cups in this card one by one, we see that Aunt Susan is wishing him continued growth (suggested by the vines growing out of one cup), peace (represented by the dove hovering above another cup), financial abundance (appearing as bubbles or coins rising from a third cup), and good luck (based on the rainbow emerging from a fourth cup). The top three cups in this card wish him magic (depicted by the stars above one cup), passion (portrayed by the fire in another cup), and spiritual vision (as depicted in the ghost-like emanation from the highest cup pictured on this card).

Amy's Channeling Session with her Spirit Guide Chryseia

Amy has always felt a strong connection with her spirit guides, and depends on them daily for protection and guidance. She has become familiar with a few of them through psychic readings, meditation, and personal experience. Amy is aware of one spirit guide who takes the form of a small child, and often appears when Amy is feeling sad or lonely. She would like to know more about this young spirit, in particular, if she is a loved one Amy knew in this lifetime, or a special guide who has traveled with her for centuries.

As a Virgo, Amy chose the Queen of Pentacles as her significator, and opted for the High Priestess (as recommended in the directions) for the significator in position 1. After shuffling, Amy drew fourteen cards and laid them out as shown in the illustration.

In the cup of the chalice (Cards 1–5), we look for confirmation that Amy is in contact with the childlike spirit guide she would like to learn more about. Here we find:

    Spirit Guide, significator 1—High Priestess
    Amy, significator 2—Queen of Pentacles
    The Lovers
    The Empress
    The Sun
    Five of Pentacles
    Three of Swords

These cards tell the story of this spirit guide. When Amy saw the cards, she realized at once that this childlike soul was the baby she had miscarried five years earlier. She was in a romantic relationship (the Lovers) and at some point, became pregnant (the Empress). She was excited about becoming a mother (the Sun) but when she was five months pregnant (confirmed by the Five of Pentacles) Amy suffered a miscarriage (Three of Swords). She named the little girl Chryseia, after her great-grandmother, and held a funeral service for her. At this point, it appears Chryseia became one of her spirit guides.

Channeling Chalice Reading
Amy's Channeling Session with Her Spirit Guide Chryseia

The stem of the chalice (cards 6–9) contains a message for Amy from Chryseia. Here we see:

Six of Cups
Seven of Cups
Three of Cups
Four of Wands

Chryseia serves as Amy's spirit guide and her main purpose is to remind Amy to play and have fun (Six of Cups). Chryseia will often appear in the most unexpected ways, whenever the worries of life start to overwhelm Amy (Seven of Cups). (Note the middle cup in this card, depicting the emergence of a veiled, fun-loving spirit.) In the Three of Cups, this spirit guide wants Amy to dance, celebrate, and enjoy life. The Four of Wands reminds Amy that when she needs to call on Chryseia, she should meet her in the atrium (as illustrated in the Four of Wands) that Amy created in her backyard in memory of the baby.

In the base of the chalice (cards 10–14), the insight and guidance Amy seeks appears. Because the reading has already answered her question about the identity of this spirit guide, these cards send additional messages from Chryseia to Amy.

These cards are:

> Five of Cups
> Wheel of Fortune
> Temperance
> The Star
> Ten of Cups

Chryseia does not want Amy to be sad because of her early demise as an infant (Five of Cups). She indicates that the miscarriage was karmic (Wheel of Fortune) and reminds Amy that Chryseia now lives with the angels (Temperance). She feels blessed to be Amy's special spirit guide, and loves the fact that because she is a heavenly form (the Star), Chryseia can be with Amy whenever she wants, to brighten Amy's life. The final card, the Ten of Cups, is Chryseia's way of sending Amy an abundance of love, joy, and blessings.

Appendix A
TAROT KEYWORDS

The Major Arcana

The Fool—New journey, innocence, trust, new beginnings
The Magician—Power, mastery, magic, deception, illusion
The High Priestess—Intuition, wisdom, psychic energy
The Empress—Creativity, nurturing, new life, mother, wife
The Emperor—Achievement, authority, success, father, husband
The Hierophant—Tradition, ritual, spiritual law, religious leader
The Lovers—Sex, love, partnership, masculine/feminine balance
The Chariot—Movement, being pulled in two directions, vehicles, speed
Strength—Strong, brave, empowered, taming the wild, animal lover
The Hermit—Introspection, spiritual seeking, illumination
Wheel of Fortune—Karma, cycles, ups and downs, chance
Justice—Truth, legal matters, fairness, justice
The Hanged Man—Suspension, being in limbo, waiting, atonement
Death—Transformation, rebirth, endings followed by new beginnings
Temperance—Patience, protection, angel or wishing card
The Devil—Trickery, fear, undermining, evil intentions
The Tower—Crisis, upset, cleansing, unexpected events, breakthrough

The Star—The wish card, dreams, magical solutions
The Moon—Psychic, illusion, night journey, dreams, full/new moon
The Sun—Energy, light, new life, relationships, radiance
Judgement—Breakthrough, answers, reckoning
The World—Culmination, end of one cycle, beginning of a new cycle, or higher education

The Minor Arcana

Wands

Focus—Business or spiritual
Element—Fire
Season—Spring
Ace—New life, inspiration, creativity, spiritual awakening
Two—Business proposal, invitation
Three—Waiting for guidance, expectant
Four—Foundation, home, redecorating, real estate
Five—Competition or conflict
Six—Entering a battle with confidence
Seven—Defending one's self
Eight—Air travel, timing card—two days, two weeks, two months
Nine—Spiritual depth, preparedness, accomplishment
Ten—Burdens, oppression, shouldering extra responsibilities
Page—Spiritual messages, business ideas or proposals
Knight—Moving with ambition, passion, and determination
Queen—Strong-willed, passionate, creative woman; Aries, Leo, Sagittarius
King—Strong-willed, passionate, creative man; Aries, Leo, Sagittarius

Cups

Focus—Emotions
Element—Water
Season—Summer
Ace—New love, emotional renewal, new passion
Two—Romance, proposal, offer
Three—Celebrations, gathering, special events
Four—Boredom, waiting for change, unexpected gift from heaven
Five—Disappointment followed by the promise of a better future
Six—Joy, past life connection, children, friends, soul mates
Seven—Illusion, addictions, worry, overwhelmed
Eight—Leaving the past behind, moving to a higher level
Nine—Indulgence, overdoing, addiction, fun, irresponsible
Ten—Love, marriage, emotional contentment
Page—Tenderness, expressions of love, messages by phone
Knight—Charming, a Casanova/Jezebel, romance
Queen—Emotional, nurturing, artistic, psychic woman; Cancer, Scorpio, Pisces
King—Emotional, nurturing, artistic, psychic man; Cancer, Scorpio, Pisces

Swords

Focus—Thoughts and intellect
Element—Air
Season—Autumn
Ace—New thought or idea, triumph
Two—Indecision, blind to the facts
Three—Sorrow, broken heart, female or heart troubles
Four—Seclusion, rest, recovery from illness
Five—Defeat, separation, divorce
Six—Passage through a difficult cycle—halfway through a process
Seven—Thievery, deception, divorce
Eight—Blocked by old mindsets, limited information

Nine—Blocked movement, waiting, insomnia, nightmares
Ten—Disappointment, ruin, back troubles, surgery
Page—Internet, phone, or text messages; ideas
Knight—Ingenuity, aggressiveness, anger
Queen—Independent, strong, intelligent woman; Gemini, Libra, Aquarius
King—Independent, strong, intelligent man; Gemini, Libra, Aquarius

Pentacles

Focus—Physical world, money
Element—Earth
Season—Winter
Ace—Gift, money, renewed health
Two—Balance, weighing one's options
Three—Internship, new career, building skills
Four—Possessiveness, isolation, hiding something, carrying extra weight
Five—Anxiety, sorrow, feeling left out and all alone
Six—Generosity, loans or gifts of money, funding coming through
Seven—Reaping what one sows, rewards of hard labor
Eight—Craftsmanship, skill in one's career, success
Nine—Abundance, wealth, security
Ten—Family, home, stability, contentment
Page—Messages by mail or e-mail, letters, checks
Knight—Change, physical movement, relocation
Queen—Solid, reliable, dependable woman; Taurus, Virgo, Capricorn
King—Solid, reliable, dependable man; Taurus, Virgo, Capricorn

Appendix B

SIGNIFICATORS

Choosing a Significator

Significator cards play an important role in directing the tarot reading to a specific person, place, situation, or object. Not only do significators enable you to focus on the subject at hand, they are a great tool for verifying answers you receive. A number of readings in this book ask for a significator.

Here are some basic guidelines to help you choose the ideal significator for your readings:

People Significators

Use the chart below to find the most appropriate match, selecting a court card (king, queen, knight, or page/knave) based on the birth sign and age of the subject of the reading. In a case in which there are two or more significators of the same astrological sign or birth month, use one of the options that follow this chart to designate an alternate significator for the additional subjects.

Age	Birth Sign	People	Significator
Child 0–18	Aries, Leo, or Sagittarius	Child Male/Female	Page of Wands
19–30	Aries, Leo, or Sagittarius	Man or Woman	Knight of Wands
Over 30	Aries, Leo, or Sagittarius	Woman	Queen of Wands
Over 30	Aries, Leo, or Sagittarius	Man	King of Wands
Child 0–18	Cancer, Scorpio, or Pisces	Child Male/Female	Page of Cups
19–30	Cancer, Scorpio, or Pisces	Man or Woman	Knight of Cups
Over 30	Cancer, Scorpio, or Pisces	Woman	Queen of Cups
Over 30	Cancer, Scorpio, or Pisces	Man	King of Cups
Child 0–18	Gemini, Libra, or Aquarius	Child Male/Female	Page of Swords
19–30	Gemini, Libra, or Aquarius	Man or Woman	Knight of Swords
Over 30	Gemini, Libra, or Aquarius	Woman	Queen of Swords
Over 30	Gemini, Libra, or Aquarius	Man	King of Swords
Child 0–18	Taurus, Virgo, or Capricorn	Child Male/Female	Page of Pentacles
19–30	Taurus, Virgo, or Capricorn	Man or Woman	Knight of Pentacles
Over 30	Taurus, Virgo, or Capricorn	Woman	Queen of Pentacles
Over 30	Taurus, Virgo, or Capricorn	Man	King of Pentacles

Or, you can choose a court card (king, queen, knight, or page/knave) based on the personality traits of the subject that most closely represents the subject. For example, if the subject is a strong, independent woman, you may choose the Queen of Swords. If you are looking at a sensitive, romantic man, you can opt for the King of Cups, etc. Use your intuition to select the card best suited to represent the person for which you are reading.

Personality Trait Guidelines

King of Wands	Passionate, driven, creative man over the age of 30
Queen of Wands	Passionate, driven, creative woman over the age of 30
Knight of Wands	Passionate, driven, creative man/woman between 18 and 30
Page/Knave of Wands	Passionate, driven, creative child under the age of 18
King of Cups	Sensitive, artistic, romantic man over the age of 30
Queen of Cups	Sensitive, artistic, romantic woman over the age of 30
Knight of Cups	Sensitive, artistic, romantic man/woman between 18 and 30
Page/Knave of Cups	Sensitive, artistic, loving child, under the age of 18
King of Swords	Intellectual, strong, independent man over the age of 30
Queen of Swords	Intellectual, strong, independent woman over the age of 30
Knight of Swords	Intellectual, strong, independent man/woman between 18 and 30
Page/Knave of Swords	Intellectual, strong, independent child under the age of 18
King of Pentacles	Grounded, stable, practical man over the age of 30
Queen of Pentacles	Grounded, stable, practical woman over the age of 30
Knight of Pentacles	Grounded, stable, practical man/woman between 18 and 30
Page/Knave of Pentacles	Grounded, stable, practical child, under the age of 18

Or, you may select one of the personality cards of the major arcana (the Fool, Magician, High Priestess, Empress, Emperor, Lovers, or Hierophant) that represents the person's personality traits or the role they are playing in the querent's life.

Major Arcana Personality Card Guidelines

The Fool	Child, entrepreneur, new friend, or naïve person
The Magician	Accomplished, magical, captivating man
The High Priestess	Highly intuitive, emotional, wise woman
The Empress	Nurturing soul, mother, or wife
The Emperor	Successful businessman, father, or husband
The Lovers	Romantic partner, man or woman
The Hierophant	Boss, religious leader, or authority figure

Finally, you can choose a court card based on the physical description of the subject as your significator. For example, if the subject is a man over thirty with dark hair and a beard, choose whichever king in your tarot deck resembles him.

Situation Significators

For readings in which the significator represents a situation, select a card that corresponds with the querent's emotional state. For example, if the querent is feeling stuck and unsure of what to do next, you might select the Eight of Swords, the Devil, or the Four of Cups to represent his or her state of mind.

For situations involving spiritual, financial, business, or creative pursuits, choose the Ace of Wands or any card from that suit which most closely represents the situation.

In matters of the heart such as love, romance, emotional balance, and family, choose the Ace of Cups or any card from that suit which most closely represents the situation.

To gain guidance about ideas, communication, education, and intellectual conflict, choose the Ace of Swords or any card from that suit which most closely represents the situation.

For direction regarding physical health, money, career, and real estate, select the Ace of Pentacles or any card from that suit which most closely represents the situation.

Object Significators

Object significators can be used in a variety of readings, such as when the querent is searching for a lost object, picking out the perfect gift, manifesting something into being, or as a key reminder of what one might need for an upcoming project, event, or travel.

To find a lost item, pick a significator card from the topics below and lay it out on the table before you start the reading. (Refer to the location card combinations for more information on finding lost objects.)

If you are trying to manifest a certain object, person, or event in your life, pick a significator card and meditate on it twice daily for ten minutes, sleeping with the card under your pillow for seven nights in a row, or until it comes into being.

To make a list of needs for a special event, select a significator card and place it on the table. Shuffle the remaining cards and draw ten. First, separate the court cards to identify those people who can obtain these items for you. Read the remaining cards for other clues or reminders of items or actions important to the event.

Depending on the deck you use, select a card containing an image of what you are looking for or one that brings the object to mind. In a reading, look for these same icons to reveal more about your question.

Wands signify spiritual or ritualistic objects such as candles, incense, or anything related to the element of fire, and the colors orange, red, yellow, and white. (Example: You might choose the Four of Wands to ask, "Where did I store those four red Christmas candles I bought on sale last year?")

Cups represent dinnerware, jewelry, bathroom or kitchen objects, or anything related to the element of water, and the colors pink, light green, light blue, and black. (Example: Picking the Ace of Cups while asking, "Where is my green peridot ring hiding?")

Swords designate electrical objects, cutlery, books, paperwork, maps and computer software, communications, anything related to the element of air, and the colors indigo, yellow, green, and purple. (Example: Selecting the Three of Swords to discover, "Where did I put those old love letters from Jim?")

Pentacles represent money, gold, boxes, plants, anything related to the element of earth, and the colors black, brown, dark green, and other earth tones. (Example: Choosing the Two of Pentacles to ask, "Where did I put those two containers I wanted to plant seeds in?")

Be creative when selecting your object significators. As shown in the example from the Decision Trees reading in chapter two, the querent picked cards to represent the three gifts she wanted to purchase for her parents. She was looking at a pair of antique silver candlesticks her mother admired, so, for this choice, she selected the Two of Wands (two representing a pair of something and wands representing the element of fire, i.e., candles). She also knew they needed a new television set, so for this option, she chose the Wheel of Fortune to represent one of her parent's favorite shows, since there aren't cards with a television on them. To represent her third gift option—a Caribbean cruise—she chose the Sun, an image reflecting the climate of their destination.

Appendix C

CARD COMBINATIONS

The following section outlines tarot cards to look for when addressing certain topics. A card's meaning can change or expand when combined with additional cards, offering new or expanded information.

For example, a querent might wonder if their daughter is pregnant. In this case, the reader should watch for mother-related cards, such as the Empress, the Three of Pentacles (a new beginning), the Queen of Pentacles (a female holding a pentacle or going through physical change), or the Sun (usually depicting a small child or baby riding a horse).

When certain groupings of cards appear, they send the reader a powerful message and clear guidance. While reading on a specific topic, if at least two of the cards in this guide appear together, you are receiving a positive response to your question. Three or more of these cards will confirm the answer. Keep in mind that the more cards you draw, the stronger the affirmation you will receive.

Relationship Card Combinations

When performing a reading specific to relationship issues, these layouts are recommended:

The Inverted Pyramid
Relationships
Crossroads
Veil/Truth
Gypsy's Mirror

New Relationship

Combinations of the following cards indicate a new relationship that is forming or will come into one's life shortly. In order for a connection to have long-term relationship potential, look for one or more affirming major arcana cards in the layout (the Lovers, Sun, Star, etc.).

Ace of Cups (New love)
Two of Cups (Invitation for a date)
Three of Pentacles (Internship/new beginnings)
Six of Pentacles (Someone generous/open to a new relationship)
The Lovers (Romance)
The Sun (Positive energy/conditions are right for a new relationship)
The Star (Dreams coming true)

Does a Person Have Romantic Feelings?

When the following cards come up in combination with each other, they verify that someone has romantic feelings for the querent:

Six of Cups (Sharing)
Knight of Cups (Person interested in romance)
Queen or King of Pentacles (indicates physical attraction)

The Lovers (Romantic intent)
The Star (Positive attraction)

When any pages/knaves appear in the reading, they indicate that the other person's interest will be expressed in one of the following ways, depending on the suit:

Page of Pentacles (Card or love letter)
Page of Swords (E-mail, text, or phone call)
Page of Cups (Phone call or in person)
Page of Wands (Overt flirtation, subtle hints)

Where to Meet a Romantic Partner

The following cards indicate the best places to meet a new romantic partner. Using these guidelines, consider the cards that fall before or after to help you narrow down the location where one is likely to meet someone.

Three of Cups (Party or celebration)
Seven or Nine of Cups (Bar or tavern)
Predominance of cups (On vacation, near water, pool, lake, a restaurant)
Predominance of wands (Karmic, chance meeting, unexpected circumstances)
Predominance of swords (Blind date, through friends, Internet personal ad)
Predominance of pentacles (Work or business activities)
Ten of Pentacles (Holidays, family gatherings, graduations)
The World (While traveling or a long-distance relationship)

If your querent would like to know when they will meet their life partner, refer to the timing cards in appendix D to estimate the time of his or her appearance in the querent's life.

Long-Term Relationships

To determine if a relationship has the potential to go the distance, look for the following cards which represent endurance, abundance, support, and commitment:

Six of Pentacles (Generosity, protection, support)
Six of Cups (Soul mates, life partners)
Seven of Pentacles (Willing to work on the relationship)
Nine of Cups (Emotional abundance)
Nine of Wands (Spiritual strength, endurance)
Ten of Cups (Emotional commitment)
Ten of Pentacles (Stability, security, growth)
Empress (Wife)
Emperor (Husband)
Hierophant (Tradition, spiritual, or legal commitment)
Judgement (Legal commitment, marriage)

Marriage Proposals

The potential for a marriage proposal can be indicated by the following card combinations:

Ace of Pentacles (Ring)
Two of Cups (Proposal)
Three of Cups (Celebration)
Three of Pentacles (New beginnings)
Ten of Cups (True love)

Soul Mate Connections

When a querent is interested to know if they have found their true soul mate, look for combinations of the following cards to appear:

Six of Cups (Soul mate card)
Ten of Cups (True and everlasting love)

Ten of Pentacles (Enduring through the ages)
The Lovers (Heart and soul-based connections)
The Sun (Life force, positive energy)
The Star (Heavenly connection)
The Wheel of Fortune (Karma, reuniting lifetime after lifetime)

When three or more soul mate cards appear alongside the Two of Cups, Two of Wands, or Two of Pentacles (indicating proposal, invitation, and balance), they will strengthen the message that this is a soul mate connection.

Reconciliation

Often, querents are curious to know if an old flame will reappear in their lives, or if they will reconcile after a recent breakup. In this case, the cards will appear in an order that outlines the ending of the relationship, as well as a new beginning. To verify that the cards are addressing a past relationship, look for Death, the Tower, or the Ten of Swords to be located near a relationship card such as the Ten of Cups or the Lovers. Then, you will want to watch for the following card combinations to indicate a reunion:

Four of Cups (Unexpected gift)
Five of Cups (Things falling apart, but with future potential)
Knight of Pentacles (Change in circumstances)
The Fool (New beginnings)
Judgement (Breakthrough)

Unhealthy Relationship Card Combinations

When one is in an unhealthy or harmful relationship, a tarot reading can help identify where the problem lies. Once revealed, it will be easier to decide what needs to change, how to protect oneself, or if it's time to detach from the relationship completely.

If you discover your querent is in an unhealthy relationship, you will need to deliver the news in combination with positive solutions, so your reading remains uplifting. Most times, the querent already knows the relationship is in trouble, and simply needs confirmation. If a querent denies there are problems or appears resistant, you can still offer suggestions of empowerment if he or she chooses to remain in the relationship.

The following card combinations will help you determine if the partnership is suffering from some of these common maladies.

Imbalance of Power in a Relationship

If one person is giving too much in a relationship, or has codependency issues, the following cards will appear:

    Two of Swords (Indecisive)
    Four of Pentacles (Holding back)
    Eight of Swords (Ignoring or unable to see problems)
    Ten of Wands (Shouldering all the burdens of the relationship)
    The Hanged Man (Waiting for the other person to direct things)

The following major arcana cards can reveal the opposite of codependence, indicating an overbearing or power-driven partner, shown by a combination of these cards:

    The Magician (Male dominance)
    The High Priestess (Female dominance)
    The Empress (Mothering or smothering)
    The Emperor (Acting as a father figure)
    The Hierophant (Acting as the authority figure)
    The Devil (Using trickery or fear to control another)

Hidden Agenda Relationship Issues

There are a number of reasons a person may be involved in a relationship without the intention of commitment. Knowing the cards that identify certain behaviors or hidden agendas can help the querent to understand where the other person is coming from, and how to protect him- or herself.

The Rebounder

The following card combinations indicate someone who has not gotten over their last breakup or is avoiding a serious relationship based on having had his or her heart broken in the past:

> Three of Swords (Broken heart)
> Four of Pentacles (Holding back)
> Seven of Swords (Deception or secrets)
> Ten of Swords (Past failure or devastation, including divorce)
> The Devil (Carrying negative emotions, inability to trust)
> The Hanged Man (On hold, resistant to moving forward)

Fickle, Commitment-phobic Person

When a person has commitment issues or continues to "play the field," you will see these card combinations appear:

> Two of Swords (Indecision)
> Two of Pentacles (Keeping one's options open)
> Three of Cups (Dating more than one person)
> Four of Pentacles (Guarded, pulled back)
> Seven of Swords (Secretive, deceptive)
> Knight of Cups (Casanova)
> The Magician (Deception)
> The Chariot (Pulled in opposing directions)
> The Hanged Man (Reluctant to commit)

Casanova or Jezebel

Look for these card combinations if you suspect a person of being a smooth-talker or Casanova or Jezebel type, simply feeding his or her own ego or telling other people what they want to hear:

> Seven of Swords (Deceptive with words)
> Page/Knave of Cups (Romantic promises)

Knight of Cups (Romantic gestures)
Queen of Cups (When the person in question is a woman)
King of Cups (When the person in question is a man)
The Magician (Influence through trickery)
The Chariot (Someone trying to move things ahead too quickly)

Infidelity

When infidelity is present in a relationship or a querent is dating someone who may be married or committed to someone else, the following cards will appear, in combination with the Lovers, Ten of Cups, or Ten of Pentacles:

Two of Swords (Indecision or going back and forth)
Three of Cups (A triangle, or secondary person involved)
Three of Swords (Someone's heart will be broken)
Seven of Swords (Lies, deception)
Eight of Swords (Blinded to the truth, in denial)
Nine of Cups (Indulgence, overdoing)
The Magician (Trickery, influence, attraction)
The Devil (Secrets, lies, evil intent)

Immature or Irresponsible

If you are involved with someone who is irresponsible or acting immaturely, there are card combinations to affirm this. If this is the case, look for these cards to appear:

Two of Swords (Indecisive)
Four of Cups (Hiding from responsibility)
Six of Cups (Childlike demeanor or interactions)
Seven of Cups (Scattered)
Nine of Cups (Indulgence, irresponsible)
Ten of Wands (Appears to be easily overwhelmed)
The Fool (Naïve, immature)

Relationship Abuse

If you suspect there is the potential for abuse, or the querent is experiencing abuse in a relationship, the following card combinations will appear:

>Five of Wands (Battles)
>Seven of Wands (Having to defend oneself)
>The Chariot (Moving in erratic ways)
>The Hierophant (Overbearing, demanding)
>The Devil (Abuse of power)
>The Tower (Short-tempered)

You can determine the type of abuse by considering the frequency of cards from each of the minor arcana suits in the layout. If the cards are predominately:

>Wands (Spiritual abuse, using religion or morals to control someone)
>Cups (Emotional abuse, withholding love or affection)
>Swords (Verbal abuse, critical and judgemental, or distant and silent)
>Pentacles (Physical abuse, battery)

Relationship Endings

When a relationship is in trouble and there is a likelihood of separation or divorce, certain card combinations will appear. These cards can also affirm if one is in the midst of a breakup or wondering if their partner has lost interest. Separation, divorce, or the breakup of a relationship could be likely in combinations of the following cards:

>Three of Swords (Broken heart)
>Five of Cups (Emotional upset, things falling apart)
>Five of Swords (Separation, divorce)
>Five of Pentacles (Sorrow, grief)
>Seven of Swords (Losing something you have)
>Eight of Cups (Moving forward alone)
>The Devil (Fear, worry, loss)

Death (Endings)
The Tower (Sudden upset)
Judgement (Divorce)

Health Issue Card Combinations

When reading for health issues, begin by asking the querent if there are any areas of concern. In doing so, you will be able to identify not only the cause, but offer solutions to any troubles. Sometimes the querent will not have any obvious complaints, in which case you will be looking for imbalances in the system that can usually be corrected with supplements or color/stone or aromatherapy treatments. (Refer to the major arcana empowerment chart, appendix E.)

Disclaimer: These definitions have been designed as a guide to match certain tarot cards to health issues you might encounter in readings and should *not* be considered a medical diagnostic tool. Advise the querent to consult a physician for all medical issues.

The best layouts for use in a health reading are:

Reasons
Inverted Pyramid
Veil/Truth
Chakra/Health

The following card combinations will provide you with an overall view of each area of the human body. At the end of this section is a complete list of the cards as they correspond to health issues.

Pentacles address foreign objects in the body, and pertain to any medications or prescriptions the querent is taking. They can indicate pregnancy, implants, transplants, or tumors. Pentacles can also reveal issues in the liver, spleen, and stomach areas.

Swords usually indicate issues with the skeletal system, back problems, tendons and joints, vision issues, or the need for surgery. Mental health issues such as ADHD, depression, or bipolar disorder will also fall under this category.

Wands can point to disorders of the nervous system, such as fibromyalgia, skin problems, the muscular system, headaches, heartburn, energy or vitamin deficiencies, as well as infection, inflammation, and anxiety.

Cups typically address the fluids in the body, including blood disorders, kidney, bowel and bladder issues, menstruation, male and female sex glands, hormones, and the immune system. Cups can also pertain to depression, mental disorders, and exhaustion.

When a major arcana card appears in the reading, it may indicate a more pressing medical problem, identified by the keyword correspondence chart below.

The Head

The Emperor rules head troubles, and will appear if this is the area needing focus. Health issues centered in the head include mental disorders (anxiety, stress, depression, scattered thoughts, etc.), headaches, hearing, vision, or sinus problems.

The following card combinations appear when addressing these issues:

HEADACHES
  Six of Swords (Chronic, migraine)
  Ten of Wands (Stress, anxiety)
  Page of Wands (Sinus, ears)
  The Hanged Man (Immobilizing pain)

Note: If your querent is having frequent headaches, they could be originating from a specific source. Watch for cards that identify vision, sinus, or hearing difficulties in your reading to discover any underlying contributors.

VISION
  Two of Swords (Difficulty seeing)
  Eight of Swords (Floaters, cataracts)
  The Fool (Rules the eyes)
  Emperor (Rules the head)

    Justice (Glasses or contacts needed for correction)
    The Hanged Man (Headache, dizziness)

Hearing
    Two of Pentacles (Inner ear imbalance, vertigo)
    Seven of Wands (Difficulty hearing)
    Page of Pentacles (Ears, ringing in ears [tinnitus], allergies)
    Justice (Out of balance, hearing aids)

Sinus, Teeth, Allergies
    Two of Wands (Sinus or allergy problems)
    Four of Pentacles (Blocked sinus, tooth pain)
    Page of Wands (Sinus, allergies)
    Page of Swords (Teeth, dental)
    Justice (Out of balance)

Mental Difficulties
    Three of Cups (Therapy, counseling, support groups)
    Four of Cups (Frustration, boredom, mental health issues)
    Four of Pentacles (Isolation, fear of people, closed mind)
    Five of Cups (Sorrow, grief, despair)
    Six of Cups (Medicine for depression, too many medications)
    Seven of Cups (Emotional upsets, phobias, confusion)
    Seven of Wands (Defensiveness, self pity, fighting for life)
    Eight of Pentacles (Medicines, supplements needed)
    Nine of Swords (Anxiety, nightmares, insomnia, sleeping disorders)
    The Hanged Man (Insomnia, immobility)
    The Tower (Sudden outbursts, anger, fear)
    The Devil (Addiction issues, paranoia, spiritual maladies)
    The Moon (Depression, delusion, fear of the dark)

The Upper Body

Health imbalances in the upper body can be identified and addressed using the following card combinations:

NECK, THROAT, AND SHOULDERS
  Seven of Pentacles (Muscle strain)
  Eight of Swords (Broken bones, cast, brace, restrictive movement)
  Ten of Swords (Skeletal)
  Page of Cups (Sore throat)
  Queen of Cups (Shoulders, neck, cold or flu)
  Hierophant (Shoulders)
  The World (Skeletal)

BACK AND SPINE
  Five of Swords (Surgery)
  Six of Swords (Chronic, or long-term pain)
  Seven of Pentacles (Muscle strain)
  Eight of Swords (Restrictive movement, back brace)
  Ten of Swords (Skeletal structure, surgery, back troubles)
  Chariot (Mobility)
  The World (Skeletal)

ARMS, ELBOWS, HANDS, FINGERS
  Seven of Pentacles (Muscle strain)
  Eight of Swords (Broken bones, restricted movement, arthritis)
  Queen of Wands (Fingers, wrists, carpal tunnel syndrome)
  Queen of Swords (Arms, elbows, arthritis)
  Queen of Pentacles (Hands)
  The Star (Hands, arms, fingers)

HEART AND BLOOD DISORDERS
   Three of Swords (Heart, blood pressure, chest pain)
   Four of Cups (Fluids, blood diseases)
   Five of Cups (Anemia)
   Eight of Wands (Blood pressure, cholesterol levels)
   Nine of Pentacles (Blood thinners, heart medications)
   Nine of Swords (Blocked arteries)
   King of Cups (Circulation, diabetes)
   The Lovers (Rules the heart)

LUNGS AND IMMUNE SYSTEM
   Two of Wands (Sinus, allergy, asthma, or breathing problems)
   Four of Pentacles (Blocked breathing, colds, pneumonia)
   Eight of Wands (Dehydration)
   Page of Wands (Sinus, allergies)
   Knight of Swords (Lungs, immune system)
   High Priestess (Rules the lungs)
   Hermit (Breathing problems, immune system)

STOMACH
   Three of Swords (Heartburn, ulcers)
   Six of Pentacles (Reactions to vitamins, supplements, and/or medicine)
   Seven of Swords (Bad eating habits, food or alcohol abuse)
   Nine of Cups (Overeating, excessive drinking)
   Ten of Wands (Sensitive stomach)
   Page of Cups (Stomach flu, food poisoning)
   Knight of Wands (Stomach pain, nausea)
   Strength (Rules the solar plexus and stomach)
   Wheel of Fortune (Digestive system)

The Lower Body

Health imbalances in the lower region of the body can be identified and addressed using the following card combinations:

PELVIS, HIPS, LEGS, KNEES, ANKLES, AND FEET
  Five of Wands (Infection, inflammation)
  Five of Pentacles (Bruises, abrasions)
  Six of Swords (Chronic, long-term pain)
  Seven of Pentacles (Muscle strain)
  Eight of Swords (Broken bones, brace, restricted movement, arthritis)
  Nine of Cups (Stress, gout, fungus)
  Ten of Swords (Skeletal structure, surgery)
  King of Wands (Knees, ankles, joints, tendons)
  King of Swords (Legs, pelvis, hips)
  King of Pentacles (Feet, Exercise)
  Chariot (Rules the legs, feet, hips, thighs, and joints; mobility)
  Wheel of Fortune (Mobility, flexibility)

KIDNEYS, INTESTINES, BOWELS, EXCRETORY SYSTEM
  Two of Cups (Kidneys)
  Four of Cups (Lack of fluids)
  Four of Pentacles (Constipation)
  Five of Cups (Diarrhea)
  Five of Wands (Infection, inflammation)
  Nine of Cups (Blood, intestines, excretory system)
  Nine of Swords (Blockages)
  Knight of Pentacles (Kidneys)
  High Priestess (Hidden, internal difficulties)
  Death (Bowels, intestines, excretory system)

Reproductive System and Sexual Organs

Health troubles involving the reproductive system and sexual organs can be determined by these card combinations:

Ace of Wands (Male reproductive organs)
Two of Cups (Breasts, pregnancy)
Three of Pentacles (Early stages of pregnancy or a period of high fertility)
Three of Swords (Female reproductive organs, infertility, menopause)
Six of Cups (Pregnancy, possible multiple birth delivery)
Six of Swords (Cesarian section birth)
Queen of Pentacles (Pregnancy)
Queen of Cups (Female fertility issues)
King of Cups (Male fertility issues)
The Empress (Breasts, reproductive organs, pregnancy)
The Lovers (Heart, reproductive organs)
The Devil (Sexual organs, sexually transmitted diseases)
The Moon (Breasts, pregnancy)

Health Correspondence Cards

The Fool—Sight, vision, eye problems
The Magician—Energy, speedy recovery
The High Priestess—Hidden, internal, lungs
The Empress—Breasts, reproductive organs, pregnancy
The Emperor—Head
The Hierophant—Shoulders
The Lovers—Heart, reproductive organs
The Chariot—Legs, feet, hips, thighs, joints, mobility
Strength—Solar plexus, stomach
The Hermit—Recovery, rest, breathing problems, immune system
Wheel of Fortune—Mobility, flexibility, digestive system
Justice—Vision loss, hearing or sinus troubles
The Hanged Man—Insomnia, immobilization, headache, dizziness

Death—Mental illness, depression, bowels, intestines, excretory system
Temperance—Slow progress, long recovery, physical therapy
The Devil—Addiction, paranoia, reproductive system, sexually transmitted diseases
The Tower—Unexpected complications, sudden change in condition, Parkinson's Disease
The Star—Hands, arms, fingers
The Moon—Breasts, pregnancy, depression, delusion, fear of the dark
The Sun—Energy, restored health, full recovery
Judgement—Change in condition, breakthrough diagnosis
The World—Skin, hair, skeletal
Ace of Wands—Optimum spiritual health, male reproductive organs
Ace of Pentacles—Optimum physical health
Ace of Cups—Optimum emotional health
Ace of Swords—Optimum mental health
Two of Wands—Sinus, allergy, asthma or breathing problems
Two of Cups—Counseling, therapy, kidneys, breasts
Two of Swords—Hidden imbalance, difficulty with vision
Two of Pentacles—Restored balance, difficulty with hearing
Three of Wands—Temporary setback
Three of Cups—Support groups, therapy, counseling
Three of Swords—Heart, female organs, infertility, bleeding, heartburn, ulcers
Three of Pentacles—Strength, physical therapy, early stages of pregnancy
Four of Wands—Hospital, physical therapy
Four of Cups—Fluids, mental health issues
Four of Swords—Bed rest, recovery
Four of Pentacles—Weight issues, constipation, isolation, breathing, tooth issues
Five of Wands—Infection, inflammation
Five of Cups—Sorrow, grief, despair, depression, anemia, poisoning, diarrhea
Five of Swords—Surgery
Five of Pentacles—Bruises, abrasions
Six of Wands—Inflammation, health battle

Six of Cups—Pregnancy, emotional issues

Six of Swords—Chronic, long-term pain; Cesarian section birth

Six of Pentacles—Vitamins, supplements, medications

Seven of Wands—Defensiveness, self-pity, resistance, hearing difficulties

Seven of Cups—Emotional upset, phobias, confusion, Alzheimer's disease

Seven of Swords—Bad habits, undermining health

Seven of Pentacles—Muscle strain, insomnia

Eight of Wands—Blood pressure, cholesterol, dehydration

Eight of Cups—Isolation, depression, breathing issues

Eight of Swords—Broken bones, brace, restricted movement, arthritis, vision troubles

Eight of Pentacles—Medicine, prescriptions

Nine of Wands—Stitches, full recovery

Nine of Cups—Food or alcohol abuse, gout, intestines, excretory system

Nine of Swords—Anxiety, depression, nightmares, insomnia, blocked arteries

Nine of Pentacles—Blood thinners, cholesterol, blood pressure medication

Ten of Wands—Nerves, headaches, muscle pains

Ten of Cups—Emotional balance, pain-free

Ten of Swords—Skeletal structure, surgery, back troubles

Ten of Pentacles—Abundant health, genetics, strong immune system

Page of Wands—Sinus, allergies

Page of Cups—Throat, colds, or flu

Page of Swords—Teeth, dental

Page of Pentacles—Ears

Knight of Wands—Stomach pain, nausea

Knight of Cups—Liver, heart

Knight of Swords—Lungs, immune system

Knight of Pentacles—Kidneys

Queen of Wands—Fingers, wrists, carpal tunnel

Queen of Cups—Shoulders, neck, cold or flu, female fertility issues

Queen of Swords—Arms, elbows, arthritis

Queen of Pentacles—Hands, fertility issues, pregnancy

King of Wands—knees, ankles, joints, tendons
King of Cups—Circulation, diabetes, male fertility issues
King of Swords—Legs, pelvis, hips
King of Pentacles—Feet, exercise, mental and physical grounding

Career and Work Card Combinations

The tarot can serve as a guide when seeking one's ideal career, looking for a new job, or wondering what field to pursue though higher education. The following card combinations will help determine in what area a person can experience the most success and fulfillment.

These cards also address common questions asked about one's job in relation to promotion, job security, or trouble with a boss or coworkers.

The ideal layouts for a career reading are:

Illuminating Star
Inverted Pyramid
Decision Trees
Crossroads

Following the card combinations is the professions correspondence list which has further information and may help you identify possible careers to investigate.

Seeking A New Job

When a new job is in the querent's future, here are the cards that affirm a new, upcoming position:

Ace of Wands (New enterprise)
Two of Wands (A job offer)
Ace of Swords (Victory)
Three of Pentacles (Internship)
The Fool (New journey)
Judgement (Breakthrough)

Job Interviews

To determine if a job interview has gone well, look for these cards to appear:

> Ace of Swords (Victorious communication)
> Two of Wands (Job will be offered)
> Eight of Pentacles (Skills)
> Nine of Wands (Experience)
> Page of Swords (Clear communication)
> Strength (Impressive interview)
> The Sun (Positive energy)

If the interview did not go well, these cards will appear:

> Two of Swords (Confusion, unclear communication)
> Five of Wands (Competing with other candidates)
> Eight of Swords (Behind the scenes influences)
> Ten of Swords (Talking too much)
> The Fool (Not enough experience)
> The Tower (Too emotional, not a good fit)

Advancement

Many querents would like to know about advancement in their current job positions. To determine if a move or promotion is in the future, look for the following cards:

> Two of Wands (Offer or promotion)
> Eight of Pentacles (Successful, skilled worker)
> Ten of Pentacles (Increase in salary)
> The Fool (New Beginning)
> The Magician (Promotion, advancement)
> The Emperor (Achievement, management position)

Job Security

When one is concerned about job security, look for the following cards to appear. If the Hierophant (Boss) card appears, pay close attention to the cards near it, as they will reveal how the boss feels about the querent and his or her work.

For affirmation of job security, look for these cards:

Two of Pentacles (Balanced effort)
Four of Wands (Stable foundation)
Eight of Pentacles (Skilled worker)
Nine of Cups (Comfort, abundance)
Ten of Pentacles (Security, stability)
The Emperor (Valued employee)
Strength (Strong position)
Hierophant (Boss)

If the querent's job is in jeopardy, the following cards will alert them of this:

Two of Swords (Indecision, mixed messages)
Ten of Swords (Loss, layoff, or dismissal)
Five of Wands (Conflicts with coworkers)
Five of Pentacles (Loss of income, sorrow)
Seven of Wands (Defending one's position)
The Devil (Fear, being undermined by another)
The Tower (Stormy times, upset)
Wheel of Fortune (Business in jeopardy)

Trouble With Authority Figures

When querents finds themselves in conflict with authority figures at work, select the Hierophant (boss) as a significator card before you begin the reading. In this way you can direct the cards to reveal how the boss feels, as well as ways in which querents might be contributing to any strife. Depending on the issues they have with each other, the following cards should clarify matters:

Four of Pentacles (Holding back, not doing one's work)
Five of Wands (Questioning authority)
Five of Cups (Boss focused on mistakes, not achievements)
Seven of Pentacles (Feeling undervalued)
Eight of Swords (Rigid mindsets, control)
Eight of Cups (Indulgence, laziness)
Ten of Wands (Overburdened employer or employee)
The Moon (Illusion, suspicion)
The Hanged Man (Not being promoted, pay or hiring freezes)
The Devil (Negative attitude or feeling)

Choosing A New Career

When one reaches a crossroads at work and is ready to change directions, a tarot reading can help determine the type of career one is best suited for, and how to make the shift. For additional insight, once you have completed a reading of this type, you may want to review the professions correspondence guide at the end of this section. The following card combinations will affirm if you are ready for change and outline the steps necessary to make it happen:

Ace of Swords (New ideas, visions)
Two of Wands (At a crossroads)
Three of Pentacles (Internship, new career)
Eight of Pentacles (Entrepreneur, starting one's own business)
The Magician (Consulting, marketing, or sales)
The World (Higher education, new degree or qualification)

PROFESSIONS CORRESPONDENCE GUIDE

The Fool—Student, intern, startup of a business
The Magician—Engineering, entertainer, doctor, metaphysics
The High Priestess—Psychic, researcher, writer, metaphysics
The Empress—Day care, catering, flower shop, teacher
The Emperor—Government job, military, manager, CEO, doctor

The Hierophant—Public duties, clergy

The Lovers—Catering/Bridal shop, matchmaker

The Chariot—Auto sales, transportation industry, driver

Strength—Athletics, body-building, personal trainer, physical therapist

The Hermit—Minister, professor, scientist, inventor

Wheel of Fortune—Gambler, high-risk operations, professor, traveler

Justice—Attorney, paralegal, court reporter, police officer

The Hanged Man—Gymnast, sports, nurse, yoga or reiki instructor

Death—Funeral director, mortician

Temperance—Mental health field, hypnotherapy, physical therapy

The Devil—Scam artist, forger, illegal activities

The Tower—EMT, paramedic, firefighter, ER doctor

The Star—Entertainment, motivational speaker, charity or nonprofit work

The Moon—Astrologer, astronomer, night work (hotels/bar)

The Sun—Travel agent, hospitality industry, landscaper, outdoor work

Judgement—Judge, arbitrator, visionary

The World—Environmental work, humanitarian causes, travel agent, import/export

Ace of Wands—Internship in spiritual work or business management

Ace of Cups—Internship in health-related work, therapy, counseling

Ace of Swords—Internship in communications, journalism, electrical work

Ace of Pentacles—Internship in banking or construction

Two of Wands—Judge, mediator, visionary

Two of Cups—Minister, couples' therapist, matchmaker

Two of Swords—Eye doctor, claims adjuster, arbitrator

Two of Pentacles—Store owner, merchant, manager

Three of Wands—Security guard, watchman, comptroller, overseer

Three of Cups—Party planner, socialite, caterer, volunteer work

Three of Swords—Heart doctor, nurse, counselor, therapist

Three of Pentacles—Builder, construction, working with hands

Four of Wands—Interior decorator, remodeler, builder

Four of Cups—Philosopher, minister, research and development

Four of Swords—Rehabilitation or physical therapist, artist, writer, visionary
Four of Pentacles—Banker, stockbroker, mortgage lender
Five of Wands—Attorney, union worker, lobbyist
Five of Cups—Plumber, lab technician, janitorial service
Five of Swords—Divorce attorney, electrical engineer, land surveyor
Five of Pentacles—Laborer, unemployed, mortician, funeral director
Six of Wands—Military, equestrian, jockey
Six of Cups—Preschool or elementary teacher, florist, writer of children's media
Six of Swords—Fisherman, professor, consultant
Six of Pentacles—Banker, loan officer, benefactor
Seven of Wands—Negotiator, defense attorney, sales
Seven of Cups—Multiple jobs, director or producer of film or TV
Seven of Swords—Salesperson, spokesperson, underground trade
Seven of Pentacles—Farmer, factory worker
Eight of Wands—Airline pilot, flight attendant
Eight of Cups—Adventure seeker, mountain climber, spiritual teacher
Eight of Swords—Bindery, printing business, researcher
Eight of Pentacles—Mastery in any chosen field
Nine of Wands—Guard, advisor, manager, CEO
Nine of Cups—Bartender, chef, food services
Nine of Swords—Restricted areas, correctional facilities, factory work
Nine of Pentacles—Landscaper, realtor, designer
Ten of Wands—Laborer, truck driver, warehouse manager
Ten of Cups—Poet, actor, artist
Ten of Swords—Surgeon, chiropractor
Ten of Pentacles—Family-owned business, investment banker
Page of Wands—Announcer, disc jockey, dispatcher, minister
Page of Cups—Minister, call center/customer service, advocate
Page of Swords—Politician, lawyer, writer, interpreter
Page of Pentacles—Teacher, messenger, librarian, production assistant
Knight of Wands—Military, firefighter, police officer, EMT
Knight of Cups—Actor, poet, writer, dancer

Knight of Swords—Electrician, advocate, politician
Knight of Pentacles—Mover, farmer, physical labor, truck driver
Queen of Wands—Teacher, veterinarian, inventor
Queen of Cups—Homemaker, mother, therapist, nurse
Queen of Swords—Model, writer, lawyer
Queen of Pentacles—Hairdresser, designer, decorator
King of Wands—Pilot, stockbroker, politician, motivational speaker
King of Cups—Musician, plumber, sailor, marine biologist
King of Swords—Model, writer, public advocate, radio or TV personality
King of Pentacles—Investments, banking, oil or gas industry

Money and Finance Card Combinations

When performing a reading on financial matters, you will find that pentacles and swords typically dominate the layout's landscape. The following are common questions one may ask about their ability to maintain, improve, or protect their financial assets.

Recommended layouts for readings regarding money or finance are:

Illuminating Star
Inverted Pyramid
Decision Trees
Crossroads

Financial Gain

Most of us would like to have more money and often find ourselves faced with financial challenges. You and your querents will be looking for direction and affirmation from the tarot that financial stability is within reach. When performing a reading focused on finances, keep an open mind and consider all the cards in the layout as guideposts and suggestions for reaching your goals.

Improving Finances

When querents ask if their finances will improve, the following cards will indicate an affirmative response:

Ace of Pentacles (New money coming)
Two of Pentacles (Financial balance)
Six of Pentacles (Having more than enough money)
Nine of Pentacles (Financial abundance)
Ten of Pentacles (Security, stability)
The Emperor (Achieving financial goals)
Strength (Determination and power)

Sources of Income

The next concern may be where this money will come from, to restore or improve their financial situations. The following cards define the source of this income:

Ace of Pentacles (Gift of money)
Two of Pentacles (Second job)
Three of Wands (Waiting for expected funds)
Four of Wands (Refinance)
Four of Cups (Unexpected funds)
Six of Pentacles (Loans, personal or institutional)
Seven of Pentacles (Budgets, reorganization of spending)
Ten of Pentacles (Borrowing from family)
The Emperor (Career advancement or change)
The Hierophant (Raise, promotion)
Death (Inheritance)
Justice (Legal or insurance settlement)
Wheel of Fortune (Lottery, karmic circumstances)

Financial Loss

Money troubles can appear in many forms, whether one is about to lose a job or has lost savings in the stock market. If you do a reading where the prospect of financial loss appears, you will want to follow up with ways in which you or your querent can recover, reclaim, or rebuild finances.

The following card combinations identify financial loss:

> Five of Cups (Sorrow, despair)
> Five of Swords (Defeat, devastation)
> Five of Pentacles (Financial loss)
> Seven of Cups (Expenses outweigh income)
> Seven of Swords (Dishonesty, stolen money)
> Nine of Swords (Blocks, inability to counteract financial loss)
> Ten of Wands (Financial burdens)
> Ten of Swords (Financial devastation)
> Death (Loss of assets)
> The Devil (Irresponsibility)
> The Tower (Unexpected financial loss)

Causes of Financial Loss

The following cards reveal root causes of financial loss. Once you have determined the problem, you can use the identifying card as a significator and perform a secondary reading to help guide you or your querent forward through the healing and reclamation process.

Here are the cards that correspond to specific types of financial loss:

> Three of Swords (Medical expenses)
> Four of Wands (Foreclosure)
> Five of Cups (Divorce, death)
> Five of Pentacles (Loss of job or income)
> Seven of Swords (Lost or stolen money)
> Eight of Pentacles (Stock market, investment or business loss)

Nine of Cups (Credit card debt, overspending)
Ten of Wands (Burdened with debt)
Justice (Bankruptcy, foreclosure)

Reclaiming Financial Balance

In a secondary reading, you may want to explore your options for rebuilding your finances. The following cards indicate the best way to cut your losses and move forward:

Ace of Wands (New commitment)
Ace of Pentacles (Fresh start)
Three of Wands (Seek professional advice)
Four of Wands (Rebuild your foundation)
Six of Wands (Diligence, determination)
Eight of Cups (Leaving the past behind, moving to a higher level)
Knight of Wands (Determination, new life, creativity)
The Fool (New beginnings, starting over)
The Magician (Transform financial woes into financial goals)
Wheel of Fortune (What goes around comes around)

Location Card Combinations

Using the cards to determine a location can come in handy when one wants direction as to where to take a vacation, the ideal spot to relocate, or in the event of searching for a person or lost object.

Because there are a number of cards in any given tarot deck that can be used as direction indicators, and because different decks contain varying illustrations, focus on the images in each card, rather than their traditional meanings.

The ideal layouts to use for location readings are:

Yes or No
Illuminating Star
Mini-Inverted Pyramid
Veil/Truth

Direction Locators

When you are considering a move, vacation, or trying to locate someone, it's best to narrow down the general direction first. For example, if someone is considering two or three different places where they would like to relocate—one south of them, one to the north, and one to the east—you may be able to narrow down their options with the cards.

To determine general direction, look for these images:

> North—The Magician, Ace of Swords or Wands, all swords or wands pointing upward
> South—The Moon, the Hanged Man, swords or wands pointing downward
> East—The Sun, all cards with people facing east or to the right
> West—The Fool, all cards with people facing west or to the left

Vacation or Relocation Locators

To determine the best place for a vacation or relocation, first consider the direction cards. Next, identify the climate or geography of the location depicted in the following cards for more clues. For example, if you are planning a summer vacation, but your family members cannot agree on where they want to go, you can perform a reading to discover which option would work the best. If one wants to go to a beach in Florida, and you live in Ohio, the south location indicator cards should come up. In addition, cards that imply bodies of water should appear. If another family member wanted to go camping in the Rockies, look for cards indicating west (if the Rockies are west of you) as well as cards depicting mountains.

> Coastal—Temperance, the Sun, Six of Swords, cards depicting water or shorelines
> Mountains—Eight of Cups, the Fool, cards depicting mountains
> Foreign country—Wheel of Fortune, the World, Nine of Pentacles
> Urban—The Moon (night life), the Chariot (traffic), the Star, Eight of Cups
> Rural—The Empress, Eight of Cups, Seven of Pentacles
> Travel by plane—Eight of Wands, the World
> Travel by car—The Chariot

Lost Object Locators

When searching for a lost object, consider the cards closely for clues. For example, if a majority of the cards contain images pointing upward (swords and wands), you need to search higher up, perhaps a second story, an attic, or high up in a closet. If icons in the image point downward, look lower, as the object may have rolled under the bed or a desk.

> Four of Wands—Object is somewhere in your home
> The Chariot—Object may be in your car or garage
> The Hermit—Object is hidden in a dark place, and may require a flashlight to find it
> Seven of Swords—Object may have been stolen or is lost for good

When the cards contain an abundance of objects, such as the Ten of Pentacles or Nine of Cups, search in an area where items tend to collect, for example, a drawer, jewelry box, or filing cabinet.

A predominance of well-dressed people (major arcana or court cards) could indicate that the object is hidden in clothing, so search in closets, pockets, or the laundry basket.

If you encounter a majority of cup cards (indicating the object is near water), look in the kitchen or bathroom.

If more wands appear in the reading, check near heating sources or a fireplace.

When most of the cards are swords, check around your computer, office space, or telephone.

Pentacles will tell you if your lost object stands alone (Ace of Pentacles) or if it's hiding amongst multiple items (Five to Ten of Pentacles), as in a drawer or filing cabinet, depending on the number pentacles depicted in the card.

Appendix D

TIMING CARDS

These guides are designed to help determine the time frame of events yet to come. When a reading predicts a certain event or change in circumstance, you or your querent will want to know the approximate timing.

There are three methods you can use, individually or in combination, to extract timing information from the tarot cards:

> Numerological timing—to verify something that should occur in a matter of days
>
> Zodiac timing—to determine what month the event will occur
>
> Minor arcana timing—to determine the week within a year's cycle

When determining timing, first consider the question as well as the event the cards are predicting. For example, if the querent has just met the partner of his or her dreams, he or she might ask if marriage is in the future. Obviously, this is rarely an event that will happen within a few weeks or months, so to determine a clear time, you will want to refer to the monthly zodiac method of timing below, or consult the minor arcana timing method that covers the fifty-two weeks of the year. Pay close attention to any repeating numbers in the reading as well. If you have more aces in the layout, you can safely assume this marriage will take place within the first year. A predominance of twos may suggest two years.

However, if the event is something that should happen within a few days or weeks, you will want to use the numerological timing method listed below.

To ask about the timing of a certain event, the following layouts are recommended:

Yes or No
Illuminating Star
Mini Inverted Pyramid
Birthday/Yearly Forecast

Numerological Timing

When a timing question revolves around something that should happen rather quickly (such as "When will I hear back about a job?" or "When will so-and-so call me?"), you will need to focus on the predominant numbers that appear in the reading. If you see a predominance of threes in the layout, you can safely predict that these calls will come in over the next three days, etc.

Be sure to include the major arcana when you research the predominant numbers. For instance, if you draw the Lovers (number six), you can include it with any additional sixes that appear in the layout.

Zodiac Timing

You can also determine timing based on current astrological influences by noting the number of cards that appear in a particular suit.

For example, if you perform a reading in July that predicts a new relationship coming your way, you might then follow up with a Yes or No reading to determine timing. When phrasing your question in the Yes or No format, you might ask, "Will this relationship appear in the next three months?" If the cards you pull result in a "no" response, you can reshuffle and ask, "In the next six months?" and so on, until you receive a "yes" response. Once you do, look at the cards overall to identify the time frame. If the reading indicated this event would happen within the next three months, and the majority of cards were swords, you would refer to the chart below to estimate that this relationship is due to appear sometime in October.

Here are the guidelines for determining timing through the zodiac:

> Wands indicate the current or sun's next cycle through a fire sign:
> Aries (April), Leo (August), or Sagittarius (December)
>
> Cups indicate the current or sun's next cycle through a water sign:
> Cancer (July), Scorpio (November), or Pisces (March)
>
> Swords indicate the current or sun's next cycle through an air sign:
> Gemini (June), Libra (October), or Aquarius (February)
>
> Pentacles indicate the current or sun's next cycle through an earth sign:
> Taurus (May), Virgo (September), or Capricorn (January)

Minor Arcana Timing

Here are the weeks of the year generally associated with the minor arcana tarot suits. You can use these tables to determine when an event might happen or select them as significators to do a reading for a certain period during the year.

WANDS
- Ace—Start of spring
- Two—4th week of March
- Three—1st week of April
- Four—2nd week of April
- Five—3rd week of April
- Six—4th week of April
- Seven—1st week of May
- Eight—2nd week of May
- Nine—3rd week of May
- Ten—4th week of May
- Page—1st week of June

Knight—2nd week of June
Queen—3rd week of June
King—End of spring

Cups
Ace—Start of summer
Two—4th week of June
Three—1st week of July
Four—2nd week of July
Five—3rd week of July
Six—4th week of July
Seven—1st week of August
Eight—2nd week of August
Nine—3rd week of August
Ten—4th week of August
Page—1st week of September
Knight—2nd week of September
Queen—3rd week of September
King—End of summer

Swords
Ace—Start of fall
Two—4th week of September
Three—1st week of October
Four—2nd week of October
Five—3rd week of October
Six—4th week of October
Seven—1st week of November
Eight—2nd week of November
Nine—3rd week of November
Ten—4th week of November
Page—1st week of December

Knight—2nd week of December
Queen—3rd week of December
King—End of fall

PENTACLES
Ace—Start of winter
Two—4th week of December
Three—1st week of January
Four—2nd week of January
Five—3rd week of January
Six—4th week of January
Seven—1st week of February
Eight—2nd week of February
Nine—3rd week of February
Ten—4th week of February
Page—1st week of March
Knight—2nd week of March
Queen—3rd week of March
King—End of winter

Appendix E

EMPOWERMENT GUIDE

The diversity of the tarot extends far beyond the art of divination. You can use the major arcana images as tools to enhance your meditation skills, access their healing properties, and empower your thoughts, actions, and spiritual awareness.

These cards can be used as amulets, carrying the power to create change in your life. Refer to the guide below to determine which gemstones, colors, and scents correspond to each major arcana image.

Meditation

Each major arcana card embodies a special message, energy, and focus. Meditating on a certain image can shift one's consciousness to promote emotional and spiritual advancement.

You can adopt a daily practice of meditating with a single tarot card, working your way through the cards numbered zero through twenty-one, or shuffling the cards and drawing one for the day. You can also select a card that addresses a specific issue on which you'd like to meditate. For instance, if you want to create more movement in your life, you would select the Chariot.

Once you've chosen your card for the meditation, refer to the chart to see what element it corresponds to. Incorporate that element into your meditation in the following manner:

Fire—Candles, incense, lava stones
Water—Water bowl, fountain, shells
Air—Incense, quartz crystal ball, feathers
Earth—Clay objects, natural stones, flowers

Next, select the corresponding color, dressing in it or adding an item of this hue to your meditation space.

Light candles or incense of the major arcana card's aromatherapy scent to complete the initial setup before you begin your meditation.

As an example, if you have chosen the Moon as your meditation card, you would incorporate a water bowl, crystal ball, or shell, perhaps wear white clothing, and light vanilla incense to prepare your meditation space.

Devote at least fifteen minutes to your meditation, focusing on the meaning of the card and its images. The card will begin to speak to you and reveal more as you concentrate on it.

Healing

Whether you are in search of physical, emotional, or spiritual healing, the images of the major arcana and their corresponding stones, colors, and scents, can evoke improvement in most areas. Wear or carry the gemstones of the matching card and surround yourself in its color with clothing, candles, or flowers. Eat more food of this color as well, and wear perfumes or light candles and incense that correspond to its signature scent.

If you are seeking physical healing, opt for cards that correspond with the element of earth, or the ones that embody the change required. The following cards work best for physical improvement:

The Empress (Self-nurturing, female troubles)
The Hierophant (Discipline, willingness)

The Chariot (Restored movement, mobility)
Strength (Recovery, improved health)
The Hermit (Rest, healing)
Temperance (Patience, steady improvement)
The Sun (Renewed energy)
The World (Fulfillment, full recovery)

For emotional healing, choose a card that corresponds with water or addresses the particular struggle you are facing. The following cards relate to emotional healing:

The High Priestess (Spiritual or therapeutic help)
The Lovers (Relationship issues)
The Hermit (Retreat, rest)
The Hanged Man (Introspection, looking inward)
Death (Grieving process, endings)
The Devil (Addressing fears)
The Tower (Anger, unfairness)
The Moon (Identifying illusions)
Judgement (Breakthroughs, new understanding)

Spiritual healing allows one to reconnect with one's true self and purpose. To evoke spiritual healing, refer to cards that correspond with the elements of air and fire. The following cards can promote spiritual healing and raise your awareness:

The Fool (New beginnings, optimism, trust)
The Magician (Help from spirit, development)
The High Priestess (Greater spiritual awareness and advancement, past life research)
The Hermit (Meditation, introspection)
The Wheel of Fortune (Karmic change, chance, destiny)
The Star (Dreams, wishes)
The Moon (Psychic powers)
The Sun (Renewed spiritual connection)

Empowerment

When you would like to strengthen certain traits in yourself to feel more empowered, you can use the major arcana to increase your resolve and character.

Pick a card that corresponds to an area of your life you'd like to improve. For example, if you have trouble handling money, or can't find a job, you would select the Emperor card. Or, if you seem unable to form a lasting relationship, the Lovers card can help improve your luck in love.

Once you have chosen the card that addresses your concerns, research the gemstone, color, and scent of this card in the major arcana empowerment chart and incorporate them into your daily life.

Each night, perform a meditation with the chosen card, and end your session by journaling about the traits of the card, listing ideas that come to you for advancement, and the progress you are making each day in pursuit of your goal.

Major Arcana Empowerment Guide

Card	Element	Keyword	Gemstones	Color	Aromatherapy
The Fool	Air	Innocence	Feldspar/Agate	White	Vanilla
The Magician	Air	Confidence	Tanzanite	Purple	Sage
The High Priestess	Water	Intuition	Quartz Crystal	Teal	Patchouli
The Empress	Earth	Creativity	Emerald	Green	Lavender
The Emperor	Fire	Achievement	Ruby	Red	Sandalwood
The Hierophant	Earth	Discipline	Topaz	Yellow	Myrrh
The Lovers	Water	Partnership	Diamond	Pink	Rose
The Chariot	Fire	Movement	Garnet	Orange	Sweet Grass
Strength	Fire	Endurance	Tiger's Eye	Yellow	Musk
The Hermit	Water	Introspection	Amber	Blue	Clove
Wheel of Fortune	Fire	Karma/Destiny	Lapis Lazuli	Rainbow	Frankincense
Justice	Air	Fairness	Turquoise	Blue	Cedar
The Hanged Man	Water	Meditation	Aquamarine	Aqua	Lilac
Death	Water	Transformation	Bloodstone	Black	Cinnamon
Temperance	Earth	Patience	Amethyst	Purple	Eucalyptus
The Devil	Fire	Fear	Obsidian	Black	Dragon's Blood or patchouli
The Tower	Fire	Release	Meteor	Red	Rain/Sea
The Star	Air	Wishes	Sapphire	Blue	Jasmine
The Moon	Water	Illusion	Moonstone	White	Vanilla
The Sun	Fire	Energy	Citrine	Orange	Citrus
Judgement	Water	Breakthrough	Jade	Yellow	Ginger
The World	Earth	Fulfillment	Opal	Green	Amber

GET MORE AT LLEWELLYN.COM

Visit us online to browse hundreds of our books and decks, plus sign up to receive our e-newsletters and exclusive online offers.

- Free tarot readings • Spell-a-Day • Moon phases
- Recipes, spells, and tips • Blogs • Encyclopedia
- Author interviews, articles, and upcoming events

GET SOCIAL WITH LLEWELLYN

www.Facebook.com/LlewellynBooks   www.Twitter.com/Llewellynbooks

GET BOOKS AT LLEWELLYN

LLEWELLYN ORDERING INFORMATION

 Order online: Visit our website at www.llewellyn.com to select your books and place an order on our secure server.

 Order by phone:
- Call toll free within the U.S. at 1-877-NEW-WRLD (1-877-639-9753)
- Call toll free within Canada at 1-866-NEW-WRLD (1-866-639-9753)
- We accept VISA, MasterCard, and American Express

 Order by mail:
Send the full price of your order (MN residents add 6.875% sales tax) in U.S. funds, plus postage and handling to: Llewellyn Worldwide, 2143 Wooddale Drive Woodbury, MN 55125-2989

POSTAGE AND HANDLING
STANDARD (U.S. & Canada):
(Please allow 12 business days)
$25.00 and under, add $4.00.
$25.01 and over, FREE SHIPPING.

INTERNATIONAL ORDERS (airmail only):
$16.00 for one book, plus $3.00 for each additional book.

Visit us online for more shipping options. Prices subject to change.

FREE CATALOG!

To order, call 1-877-NEW-WRLD ext. 8236 or visit our website

The Gilded Tarot
Art by Ciro Marchetti
Companion book by Barbara Moore

A classic Tarot deck that dazzles! Heralding archetypal elements of traditional Tarot, The Gilded Tarot is teeming with shimmering, classic imagery. High priestesses in flowing robes, wise emperors, knights on majestic steeds, mystics wielding magical tools, and other intriguing characters from medieval times abound in the Major and Minor Arcanas. This richly colored, easy-to-use deck also features standard symbols for the card suits—swords, cups, wands, and pentacles—which provides universal appeal.

This kit also includes *The Gilded Tarot Companion*, a clear and insightful guidebook to the deck's structure and each card's significance.

978-0-7387-0520-0
Boxed kit (5 3/16 x 8) includes a 78-card deck and 168-pp. book $24.95

TO ORDER, CALL 1-877-NEW-WRLD
Prices subject to change without notice
Order at Llewellyn.com 24 hours a day, 7 days a week!

Universal Tarot
Art by Roberto De Angelis

Drawn according to the instructions of the famous occultist Arthur E. Waite, the Universal Tarot provides the student with a useful working deck. Readers will recognize familiar scenes while being delighted by De Angelis's uncluttered adaptations and sophisticated use of color. Unlike the Marseilles-style decks, descriptive scenes conducive to storytelling adorn all the pips. The pictures make learning the meanings of the cards easier and help trigger the intuition and imagination. From the boundless joy of the Three of Cups, to the inexpressible torment of the Nine of Swords, to the quiet dignity of the Hermit, this deck simply and beautifully expresses the vastness of life's experiences and provides guidance via the wisdom of one of the greatest occult writers in history.

978-0-7387-0007-6
Boxed deck includes a 78-card deck and booklet $22.95

TO ORDER, CALL 1-877-NEW-WRLD
Prices subject to change without notice
Order at Llewellyn.com 24 hours a day, 7 days a week!

Lo Scarabeo Tarot
Art by Anna Lazzarini

For the first time, three tarot traditions—the Marseille, the Waite-Smith, and the Crowley-Harris—have been combined into one deck! This dynamic blend offers themes and symbols from the most influential decks in the history of tarot.

978-0-7387-1229-1
Boxed deck includes a 78-card deck and booklet $22.95

Shadowscapes Tarot
Art by Stephanie Pui-Mun Law
Companion book by Stephanie Pui-Mun Law and Barbara Moore

Renowned fantasy artist Stephanie Pui-Mun Law has created a hypnotic world of colorful dragons, armored knights, looming castles, and willowy fairies dancing on air—a world of imagination and dreams.

Lovingly crafted over six years, this long-awaited deck will delight all tarot enthusiasts with its wondrous blend of fairy tales, myth, and folklore from diverse cultures around the world. Featuring breathtaking watercolor artwork that fuses Asian, Celtic, and fantasy elements within the Rider-Waite structure, each exquisitely wrought card draws upon universally recognized symbols and imagery. A companion guide also presents evocative stories and insightful interpretations for each card.

978-0-7387-1579-7
Boxed kit (5³⁄₁₆ x 8) includes a 78-card deck and 264-pp. book $28.95

TO ORDER, CALL 1-877-NEW-WRLD
Prices subject to change without notice
Order at Llewellyn.com 24 hours a day, 7 days a week!

THE ROBIN WOOD TAROT
ART BY ROBIN WOOD

Tap into the wisdom of your subconscious with one of the most beautiful tarot decks on the market today! Reminiscent of the Rider-Waite deck, the Robin Wood Tarot is flavored with nature imagery and luminous energies that will enchant you and the querant. Even the novice reader will find these cards easy and enjoyable to interpret.

Radiant and rich, these cards were illustrated with a unique technique that brings out the resplendent color of the prismacolor pencils. The shining strength of this tarot deck lies in its depiction of the minor arcana. Unlike other minor arcana decks, this one springs to pulsating life. The cards are printed in quality card stock and boxed complete with instruction booklet, which provides the upright and reversed meanings of each card, as well as three basic card layouts. Beautiful and brilliant, the Robin Wood Tarot is a must-have deck!

978-0-87542-894-9
Boxed deck includes a 78-card deck and booklet $19.95

TO ORDER, CALL 1-877-NEW-WRLD
Prices subject to change without notice
Order at Llewellyn.com 24 hours a day, 7 days a week!

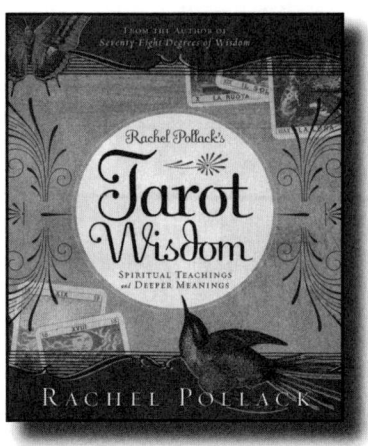

Rachel Pollack's Tarot Wisdom
Spiritual Teachings and Deeper Meanings
Rachel Pollack

Beloved by nearly half a million tarot enthusiasts, Rachel Pollack's *Seventy-Eight Degrees of Wisdom* forever transformed the study of tarot. Finally—after thirty years—the much-anticipated follow-up to this revered classic has arrived! Enhanced by author's personal insights and wisdom gained over the past three decades, *Rachel Pollack's Tarot Wisdom* will inspire fans and attract a new generation of tarot students.

Alive with a rich array of new ideas, yet reverent to the history and tradition of tarot, *Rachel Pollack's Tarot Wisdom* is a comprehensive guide for all levels. All seventy-eight cards are explored from fresh angles: tarot history, art, psychology, and a wide variety of spiritual/occult traditions. Pollack also takes tarot reading in new and exciting directions—spanning predictive, psychological, magical, and spiritual approaches. Featuring a wealth of new spreads, anecdotes from the author, and innovative ways to interpret and use tarot, this all-encompassing guide will reinvigorate your practice.

978-0-7387-1309-0
480 pp., 7½ x 9⅛ $24.95

TO ORDER, CALL 1-877-NEW-WRLD
Prices subject to change without notice
Order at Llewellyn.com 24 hours a day, 7 days a week!

Tarot Theory and Practice
Ly de Angeles

In this groundbreaking book, Ly de Angeles shares her own original ideas on the nature of prophecy and using tarot to predict the future.

Exploring quantum physics, free will, and fate, de Angeles poses a bold new theory, suggesting tarot can impact your reality . . . and your future. She also introduces Time, the god of tarot, and reveals insightful correlations between tarot and the Kabbalah Tree of Life, astrology, and the four elements. Sprinkled throughout are exercises and personal case histories that illuminate these complex ideas.

Ly de Angeles also offers guidance for putting theory into practice, along with card interpretations and sample spreads. There's advice for handling the deck, timing events, and giving accurate readings. Also included are tips for going professional: setting up a space, maintaining confidentiality, reading objectively and responsibly, communicating bad news, staying safe, avoiding burnout, and much more.

978-0-7387-1138-6
312 pp., 7½ x 9⅛ $16.95

TO ORDER, CALL 1-877-NEW-WRLD
Prices subject to change without notice
Order at Llewellyn.com 24 hours a day, 7 days a week!

Tarot Tells the Tale
Explore Three-Card Readings Through Familiar Stories
James Ricklef

Through familiar stories learn nuances of reading tarot that will help you answer any question. What if Scarlett O'Hara came to you for a Tarot reading, asking if Rhett was coming back to her? Or, if Abraham Lincoln wanted insight into the Civil War?

Peer over the shoulder of a Tarot master as he demonstrates the art of doing Tarot readings to answer a variety of client questions. Through sample readings for famous characters from history, myth, and fiction, you will discover different ways to interpret personal cards, read reversed cards, construct a good question, and even rephrase less-than-ideal questions. Explore the many permutations of the basic three-card spread, as well as how to break the common Celtic Cross into mini spreads. As a result, you will find that your readings will become more cohesive, coherent, and convincing.

978-0-7387-0272-8
288 pp., 6 x 9 $16.95

TO ORDER, CALL 1-877-NEW-WRLD
Prices subject to change without notice
Order at Llewellyn.com 24 hours a day, 7 days a week!